John D Rockefeller

The Wealthiest Man in American History

(Advice and Words of Wisdom on Building and Sharing Wealth)

Monty Gray

Published By **John Kembrey**

Monty Gray

All Rights Reserved

John D Rockefeller: The Wealthiest Man in American History (Advice and Words of Wisdom on Building and Sharing Wealth)

ISBN 978-1-77485-657-4

No part of this guidebook shall be reproduced in any form without permission in writing from the publisher except in the case of brief quotations embodied in critical articles or reviews.

Legal & Disclaimer

The information contained in this ebook is not designed to replace or take the place of any form of medicine or professional medical advice. The information in this ebook has been provided for educational & entertainment purposes only.

The information contained in this book has been compiled from sources deemed reliable, and it is accurate to the best of the Author's knowledge; however, the Author cannot guarantee its accuracy and validity and cannot be held liable for any errors or omissions. Changes are periodically made to this book. You must consult your doctor or get professional medical advice before using any of the suggested remedies, techniques, or information in this book.

Upon using the information contained in this book, you agree to hold harmless the Author from and against any damages, costs, and expenses, including any legal fees potentially resulting from the application of any of the information provided by this guide. This disclaimer applies to any damages or injury caused by the use and application, whether directly or indirectly, of any advice or information presented, whether for breach of contract, tort, negligence, personal injury, criminal intent, or under any other cause of action.

You agree to accept all risks of using the information presented inside this book. You need to consult a professional medical practitioner in order to ensure you are both able and healthy enough to participate in this program.

Table Of Contents

Introduction 1

Chapter 1: The Early Years Of John Rockefeller..4

Chapter 2: The Birth Of A Business Tycoon...15

Chapter 3: The Oil Business 27

Chapter 4: Standard Oil 34

Chapter 5: Domestic Problems Follow John From New York.......................52

Chapter 6: Rockefeller, Philanthropist 56

Chapter 7: Retirement, Rockefeller's Last Years, And His Legacy..............61

Introduction

Author was an entrepreneur. He was also philanthropist. He is believed to have been the first billionaire. His life is shrouded within mystery and mysticism. Rockefeller is associated in many legends. He was called "the Devil by his business partners" because of his hard work. His name was so scary that it scared children. Rockefeller was proud all through his life not only of his position but also of his impeccable morality.

Author was created on July 8,1839 in New York, USA. John was primarily raised by his mom, a Baptist pastor who encouraged him to work hard from childhood.

He is one American businessman who is most known for founding the Rockefeller Foundation, Standard Oil Company, and many others. He also set up charitable foundations that support education and science. His fortune was 1.53% of America's entire income at one time.

There are many world records. They include weight, speed. height. depth. But if "World Record for Wallet Thickness," was included in this world records book, then it would have been the Rockefellers.

Five Rockefeller brothers are currently in control of 88 billion USD.

These 88 trillion dollars are housed in the armored vaults of Manhattan Island's rocky foundation. On Manhattan Island lies the central part.

It was here that the Rockefeller Brothers Empire established its central headquarters. These vaults truly are a miracle in modern technology. Imagine long, narrow galleries that run several floors below ground. These are the entrances to thick, multi-layered steel chambers.

These chambers are sealed by steel doors of 52 tons that can be opened remotely. Many treasures are hidden in these concrete chambers.

Wall Street is home to the Rockefeller offices. Rockefellers opted for Wall Street as their headquarters in an effort to outsmart fashion.

They were not content to be second and built a 70-storey skyscraper with steel and glass.

But, they refused to leave Wall Street. The street just adjacent to Wall Street provided the solution. They bought a large piece of land on which they built a skyscraper. This was where the Rockefeller Bank headquarters was located.

The corridors of this skyscraper with 70 storeys are not measured in meters. Instead, they are measured in kilometers.

Chapter 1: The Early Years of John Rockefeller

"I don't believe there is any other quality more essential to success than perseverance. It can conquer almost all things, even nature." Rockefeller

Rockefeller - "The most important for a young woman is to establish an credit -- a history, character."

It would be difficult not to have a father with the title "Devil Bill", and have that father make an indelible mark on your childhood. John Davison Rockefeller was the son of William Avery Rockefeller's and Eliza

Davison Rockefeller's, who were born in Richford (New York), on July 8, 1839. Bill Rockefeller's influence was profound on both his son's conduct of business and his personal life.

According to family legends John Rockefeller and Lucy Rockefeller were the first to settle in upstate New York. John's grandmother Lucy Rockefeller would not allow them to move any further west. Lucy opposed the idea of their moving on to Michigan from her husband Godfrey. Godfrey called the steep hill in Richford, Michigan "Michigan Hill" and stated that it was the nearest he would ever come to Michigan.

Richford, at the time John was conceived, was still close to being the Iroquois home. Richford had a few other things in common with the Iroquois town: a sawmill, farm land and a whiskey distillery. Devil Bill's lifelong habit of disappearing from the scene for prolonged periods of times and leaving no trace of his location was established by this time. But, he often returned to Richford with large amounts of cash that were displayed for all to see. The money was what motivated his decision for Eliza Davison to marry him. All the signs pointed towards Bill marrying Nancy Brown. He charmed Eliza upon his arrival on her father's porch. He presented himself to Eliza as a charming, smartly-dressed, peddler for trinkets. He claimed to be deaf mute. Later, he said that it made other people feel more comfortable sharing secrets in his presence. Eliza made a statement one day saying that she would marry Bill provided he was not "deaf, dumb," although she later realized that Bill's truth was often elusive to her. Eliza's own father sensed this and protested their engagement. Bill was driven by the fact that Eliza was going to receive $500 from his father on her marriage.

Eliza quickly realized that Bill was not the right man for her life. The Davison's were an upper-middle class family. The Rockefellers were poor, and could even be called hillbillies. It was hard enough for Eliza to feel the shock of having to move from her comfortable farmhouse to a plain two story clapboard house built on top of a hill. However, Eliza quickly realized that Nancy Brown would be living in her house. Bill brought his "housekeeper" with him to Richford to stay with him and his bride. It was an important step in planting his mistress and his wife under the same roof.

Devil Bill

Within a year of Eliza's marriage, Bill had started to have children with both women. Eliza gave up a child in 1838 when Lucy, Eliza's daughter, was born. In 1838, Nancy gave birth, and Clorinda was born. Clorinda never lived to be an adult. Nancy gave rise to Cornelia a few weeks after John was conceived in 1839. Eliza followed with the births William, Jr., Mary, Franklin, Frances, as well twins named Frances.

William Avery Rockefeller Jr.

Author Rockefeller's frugality and meticulous recordkeeping of expenses are part of his legend. But, while his father seemed to inspire him, it was his mother that instilled in him the importance to save. Bill frequently left his family to go on his adventures. He never said where he was heading or when he would be back. Eliza never knew when his line of credit Bill had opened for his family at his general store. She needed to make sure that the money lasts.

Bill was often rich and able to pay his bills at the general stores when he returned. Bill, despite his many faults, always paid his bills promptly and instilled the same value in his son. Eliza was never too relieved to meet him. She would only do her best to welcome him back to her home. Over the years, however, the strain on her skin began to show.

John's neighbor called his father "Devil Bill" as he was both fascinating and mysterious to them. Was he a thief or a criminal? Was he an escaped desperado? Even though everyone knew that Bill had been away from his family for many years, many people found themselves drawn to his stories upon his return. The Rockefellers were not afraid to host a big dinner for Bill while he entertained Richford's family with his grand stories.

Devil Bill was actually a conman. While he may have won money from contests shooting, most of his earnings came from scamming people out their cash. One method was to sell trinkets, jewelry and other items for high prices. Other times, he was a con man who made his money by defrauding people out of their cash. He claimed that a potion or tonic could cure any number if ailments. Many times, the so called medicine was little more that alcohol. Even trained physicians would resort to treatment that was primitive if certainly not barbaric. Bill Rockefeller toured the West and claimed to be a doctor. It was three decades since George Washington died of strep throat. Washington's doctors tried to cure the infection by draining five pints out of his blood. Factoring in the fact that rural areas had virtually no medical care, it wasn't surprising people would pay money to use Devil Bills herbal remedies. Devil Bill was so proud of his career that he advised his family to "trade dishes with platters". He also said, "I cheat boys every chance" I want to make 'em sharp."

John was 3 years old when Devil Bill moved his family to Moravia. They quickly realized that Moravia had a different lifestyle than Richford. Eliza's father lived three miles from the small village, making it a more established community. Bill's long absences were less difficult for her to cope with, as her father was easily reachable if necessary. John was a serious, intelligent child. He seemed older than his years. Eliza relied on John more as he grew older. John was not the best student of his siblings. However, John had more education that most American children in mid-century America. He also seemed to be a natural entrepreneur. At age 8, he was responsible to purchase cordwood and took great care that he was only purchasing the best.

John was 10 years when the Rockefellers started moving again. Bill was indicted again for raping Anne Vanderbeak. Eliza had contracted Vanderbeak to help manage their growing household. According to July 1849 records, the incident occurred May 1, 1848. The indictment was issued in July 1849. Although the facts of the assault remain a mystery, it should be remembered that it was difficult for anyone to accuse of rape. Bill fled Oswego with his relatives before he could be charged or arrested. Although it is unclear why Bill was not arrested, law enforcement may not have pursued him.

Oswego is found near the Pennsylvania-New York border. This town was much more established than Moravia. The serene setting on the lake was beautiful. John didn't believe his father had taken the family from Oswego to escape rape accusations. That is not surprising considering John grew angrier over the years and developed the ability of ignoring the bad things. John did not deal with negativity unless it was necessary. Vanderbeak and John were the only people John knew.

Despite their reasons for being there the Rockefellers lived happily in Oswego. However their stay was only three years. John would not discover that his father was absent on another of his travels for many years. But he had a completely new life and new identity. Devil Bill became Doctor William Levingston. His charming charms won the affection of Margaret Allen from Ontario, 17 years old. Margaret Allen and her family were quite attracted to "Dr. Levingston did not know that the doctor had been a married conman and that he had children back in Oswego. But, Bill, 42, was married to Margaret Nichols, New York on June 12, 1855. In addition to being accused of rape and having two other children, he was also an avid bigamist.

Margaret's daily life would not be very different from Eliza or the children. It's not clear if Margaret, the new bride, found it odd that Bill saw her only once a month. However, Bill had clearly never intended to abandon his first family in order to marry Margaret. He apparently intended to keep them together secret and at this point, Devil Bill moved Eliza with the children once more to Cleveland. It is possible that Devil Bill planned on maintaining two households because Cleveland is separated from Ontario only through Lake Erie. However, he began to leave Eliza and his role as Bill Rockefeller over time. John didn't leave John's home, but John made it clear that Margaret would never be discovered by his mother.

Chapter 2: The Birth of a Business Tycoon

Rockefeller: "If it is your desire to succeed, you must seek new avenues rather than continue on the same paths of success."

"I can think about nothing more pleasurable that a lifetime devoted to pleasure," - Author Rockefeller

John saw the immediate consequences of Devil Bill taking on a second parent. John's plans of attending college ended when his father wrote to John saying that John needed work. John dropped out with just two months left to graduate high school.

John felt the best decision he could have was to get into business. Folsom's Commercial College hosted him for three months in the spring of 1855. He took a course in bank and bookkeeping. The $40 cost was an initial investment in the life of the man who would go on to become a millionaire and the most wealthy person in the country within a decade.

Author Rockefeller celebrated "Job Day" for the majority of his adult life. September 26, 1855 was when he was first hired to work as a bookkeeper in Hewitt and Tuttle's Cleveland-based produce shipping and commission merchant company. Rockefeller spent a lot of time searching for a job. Rockefeller didn't want to work in small companies and instead sought out larger corporations with potential for advancement and capital that would pay fairly. It took six weeks to get the job. His father suggested that he might have the option of living at home, but he was determined to find work. Rockefeller was determined that he would make it on his terms and not be controlled by his father.

Rockefeller didn't care that Rockefeller started work immediately upon his hire at Hewitt and Tuttle. He wouldn't receive any pay for the three first months, since it was not uncommon at the time to accept a unpaid apprenticeship. Rockefeller must have proven his worth because he was awarded $50 back pay on December 31 and also informed by his employer that his wages would be increasing to $25 per week, effective immediately. John Rockefeller, aged 16, was able to leave his dysfunctional father's home with money in his pockets and a modest room at the local boardinghouse.

Rockefeller 18 years ago

Rockefeller also purchased the legendary Ledger A. Rockefeller purchased LedgerA for 10c. He used the ledger almost obsessively to keep track of every penny earned and every dollar spent. He bought Ledger A to fill in the gaps and renamed it Ledger B. It was a routine that Rockefeller never stopped following, and one that he passed on as a legacy to his children. Rockefeller kept LedgerA all his life. It was something that nearly brought him to tears, even years later when he was a millionaire.

Rockefeller had a tendency to be more focused on making money and being successful at work the more he was successful. He would sometimes not get home until 10:00 pm, and he often arrived at Hewitt and Tuttle's office by the Cuyahoga River. He tried to strike a bargain with himself to limit his work hours but this was not a successful strategy. He loved the work. Even though it was monotonous and tedious, it was still enjoyable for him. Rockefeller once said that "Singleness and purpose are the main essentials to success in all areas of life, no mater what your aim may be." Rockefeller enjoyed bookkeeping and numbers. His persistent nature made him a valuable bill collector. Rockefeller only feared that he would not be able pay the

rent due on company properties.

Eliza Rockefeller raised children to be Baptists and to follow strict religious principles. John never drank alcohol. As an adult, he would be a strong supporter of temperance. John was not able to enjoy opera and theater. He preferred the Erie Street Baptist Church. Later, it was renamed Euclid Avenue Baptist Church. Rockefeller received his baptism in 1854 at this church. He also served as a Sunday school teacher and janitor. Rockefeller raised $2,000 in order to save the church from being bankrupt.

Rockefeller appreciated the fellowship and brotherhood offered by church. Even in his later years, he found comfort in the church. He said once, "This Sunday School was of help to [me], greater perhaps than any other force of my Christian faith, and I can only ask no better for you than this: that you, and all the others who shall follow you in that great band for Christ, shall be granted the same measure as I have been allowed to enjoy." He also said, "[W]e don't have to get old to learn the Bible." Each lesson provides new meanings and new insights that will make us better.

Rockefeller used religious principles when it came to money. He said repeatedly that God wanted Rockefeller to make as many money as possible in order to be able and give as much of his wealth to others. Rockefeller understood that the money he made was God's. He was simply acting as the steward. Rockefeller's income was very modest at just a dollar a daily. He still gave as much or as high as six percent to charity, which increased to ten per cent as he entered his twenties. His philanthropy was not restricted to the church at such a young age. He gave money to an African American man to help him buy his wife free from slavery. Rockefeller, a staunch believer in the abolition of slavery, was delighted to do so.

Devil Bill was busy working for Hewitt or Tuttle. He asked him for his supervision of the building of Eliza and the Cleveland children's home. Rockefeller, who spent a lot of his adulthood putting a positive spin and using euphemisms to describe his father's exploits and putting a positive spin upon negative situations, later stated that his dad was showing him trust, and giving him responsibility. Most likely, Bill did not invest his time in overseeing construction. This marked the beginning for his transition away from being William Rockefeller's husband to Eliza and into Dr. William Levingston who was married to Margaret. Bill expressed his gratitude to his son when the house was finally completed by charging rent to live inside it.

Rockefeller requested a raise to $800 per the year from Hewitt. When Hewitt told him that he could only offer $700, Rockefeller accepted a partnership in an commissions merchant business with Maurice B. Clark. Clark and Rockefeller arranged to put $2,000 into the firm to get it up and running. While Rockefeller saved $1,000, Clark left him short by $1,000. Rockefeller took out $1,000 from his father to make the firm a success, paying 10 percent interest. However, he was eager to be his own boss. Rockefeller would not work for anyone again.

Rockefeller was not yet twenty-one when he left Hewitt and Tuttle. He was grateful for all the knowledge he had acquired, but he was ready and able to take over as a partner with Clark and Rockefeller at 32 River Street. Their office overlooking Lake Erie was perfect for commodities. It was also a profitable business in an area populated by Northeastern residents looking for new business opportunities. Clark and Rockefeller traded in all manner of goods, including meat, grains, hay, and salt. Their first year brought in $450,000. In 1860 their profits were barely over $4,000 and in the Civil War the profits shot up by $17,000 the next year.

Rockefeller's business sense is a major factor in Rockefeller's financial success. Rockefeller, who was also a third partner in the partnership, did not operate in the same fashion as Clark and George Gardner. Clark and Gardner enjoyed spending their profits. Rockefeller on the other hand, who is a thrifty individual, thought it crazy to spend money on $2,000 yachts. Gardner suggested a Sunday afternoon getaway and Clark objected to such a purchase. Gardner once said that he thought you liked money more than all other things in the world. Rockefeller believed business was more fun than business. Gardner was resigned from the firm in 1862. Rockefeller would never write about him or speak of him again.

Rockefeller was making plans to become a business mogul, but the country was falling apart and the issue regarding slavery could only be solved through war. Rockefeller was an undisputed abolitionist like many Clevelandans. He was also a Union scion whose first vote for Abraham Lincoln was in 1861. Rockefeller was a wealthy man who paid $300 for a replacement to fight in his place after the Confederates attacked Fort Sumter. J.P Morgan (a fellow industrialist tycoon) did the same, as Teddy Roosevelt's grandfather.

The Civil War was more than a time for combat, it was a chance for Rockefeller's to make some money. He understood this well: "The only way you can make money is to purchase when blood is running down the streets." The commodities business was strongly tied to war. Clark and Rockefeller were likened to war rooms where men stopped by to find out the latest developments. Frank Rockefeller served in World War I, and he did not fight. However, he had to lie to his age about it as he was only 15. John thought it strange that Frank would be willing to go to battle when he could have his money. Frank, however, was a different kind of person. Frank was outgoing and social while John was focused, serious, and stoic. Frank had youthful fantasies about war and was more open to the possibility. John paid for Frank's uniforms, guns, and provisions so that Frank could fight. However, he did not want to do so. These were some of the initial stages of Frank and John's long-lasting disagreements that would end in Frank refusing to speak with his brother.

Frank Rockefeller

Union won because of its superior railroad network. The South's industrial power could never match that of the North. Of course, this meant that commodity prices shot up, and Clark and Rockefeller made tremendous profits on food and farm equipment. Rockefeller was also looking at other ventures and the profits from war gave him capital. Rockefeller was open to investing in oil.

Chapter 3: The Oil Business

Rockefeller - "The ability or ability to deal effectively with people are as easily purchasable commodities as sugar or caffeine and I will be paying more for that ability."

"I believe strongly in the dignity and worth of labor, regardless of whether it is with head or with hand. I believe that the world owes none man a living, but gives every man the opportunity to make his living." – Author Rockefeller

Rockefeller worked until the wee hours at Hewitt-Tuttle by way of a lamp powered only by whale oil. While this was a common source to light the room in the late 1850s, it was too expensive for most people. Although there were other options available, such as cottonseed or lard oil, crude wicks coated in fat and crude wicks, none were considered reliable nor safe. As industry and business grew, so did the desire for low-cost lighting that would allow factories and offices to remain open all hours. That was made possible by the discovery and use of rock oil in western Pennsylvania.

Rockefeller convinced Maurice Clark that he would join him in the business of oil with a chemist called Samuel Andrews. Andrews brought the scientific brain, while Rockefeller was more business-oriented. Cleveland would become home to 30 oil refineries by the end of two years. Rockefeller was optimistic about the opportunity that the oil boom presented, and he encouraged his partners to keep expanding their interests, even though it meant borrowing money.

Clark and his siblings, who had already been brought aboard as partners, did however not share Rockefeller's enthusiasm. Clark and his brothers made numerous threats to dissolve the partnership. However, Rockefeller responded with open arms. Rockefeller had already begun to set the wheels for the dissolution. He was sick of having the Clark brothers debate decisions that were in the best interests the business. Andrews was able to make a secret agreement with him and agreed that he would join him when the partnership ended. He then just waited. Rockefeller knew it would be only a matter if he and Clark brothers dissented again. Rockefeller was ready to accept it when it happened in early 1865. Rockefeller accepted the dissolution offer. The Clark brothers couldn't believe what they were hearing, so Rockefeller was asked if that is what he wanted. It was. Rockefeller, already having funding lined up from local bankers, suggested an open auction. The highest bidding bidder would own the majority of the company. Clark and Rockefeller fell apart on March 2, 1865 when their bid of $72,500 was successful. Rockefeller and Andrews Oil Company quickly built a reputation for being one of America's largest oil refineries. Their capacity to refine 500 barrels per hour was more than double that of its closest competitor.

John Rockefeller must prove that he is capable of providing a stable income and a comfortable life in order for Laura "Cettie", Spelman to love him. However, his business operations would require his constant support. John and Cettie matched perfectly for these reasons.

Rockefeller met Laura Spelman at high school, which was a nickname for Cettie.

Cettie had been in business classes at the time, which was somewhat unusual, but not surprising, given her position as class valedictorian. It was even more surprising, considering her commencement speech which was a nod toward the women's empowerment movement, "I Can Paddle My Own Canoe."

Cettie

The Spelman's, while not as wealthy than other families who sent their kids to Central High School, were well off. Cettie's father Harvey Spelman is a well-respected Cleveland businessman and philanthropist. He was elected to Ohio's legislature on 1849, and helped create an Akron Congregational congregation. Cettie had a Baptist upbringing and a strong belief about abolition. Spelman house even served as a stop on Underground Railroad. This route helped slaves escape and free them. Rockefeller would name Spelman college, the first liberal-arts college for black women, in Atlanta, in honor of his wife.

Cettie demanded that her future husband could provide for her needs. John and Cettie had similar views of the world. Cettie was happy and supported John's notion of wise spending. While she believed in God and the church, nothing was more important to her than God and her faith, she did not force her beliefs onto others. Cettie was an even-tempered person with an interest in music, literature and art. Cettie was a teacher. She didn't have to be married to continue her teaching career. In fact, many of her female students wept on her last day of teaching.

John and Cettie had not yet been engaged by 1862. There are some signs that another suitor is involved. Rockefeller however, got her attention with an outrageous splurge that was totally out of character for him. A $118 diamond engagement-ring. Cettie, after nine years together, was finally married to John at the Spelman residence in

Cleveland on September 8,1864. John spent his morning at work, but only revealed his plans in the afternoon when the 26-strong staff were invited to a special luncheon. On his way out, he informed the manager that everyone should have fun at lunch but that they had to return to work.

John and Cettie were able to spend a month together in Niagara Falls and Montreal. Then they moved into Eliza's home where they stayed for the first six years of their marriage. They built their two-story brick home just down the street. Cettie gave up the Clark siblings in 1865 when Rockefeller purchased them. In that year, Elizabeth was born, which is what everyone knows as Bessie.

Rockefeller, with his family at his side, began to develop his plan to expand the business.

Chapter 4: Standard Oil

Rockefeller: Competition is a sin

Do you know what the only thing gives me pleasure? It's watching my dividends coming into." - Author Rockefeller

Post-Civil War America had many prosperous times. America was known for its ability to produce large quantities of industrial goods, with oil being the most promising. Many veterans came from all walks of life to explore the possibility of oil speculation. However few of them had as much business acumen as Rockefeller. Sam Andrews, Rockefeller and Standard Works opened a second Cleveland refining plant. William was dispatched to New York City to open a New York office to keep John informed of the importance of the export market. Rockefeller was 26 when he had laid the foundations to his oil empire.

Andrews and Rockefeller introduced Henry Flagler to Andrews on March 4, 1867. They did so thanks to a handsome loan from Stephen V. Harkness. Flagler, a dapper and energetic man 10 year older than Rockefeller, was an old friend of Rockefeller's who shared his love for making money. He also made his way through Civil War service, selling grain to alcohol distillers. He entered the salt trade, but lost so little money that he was forced to skip lunch. Flagler never lost his desire to take on risks and was well aware of the dangers involved in being too satisfied. Flagler's friendship with John Rockefeller led to a close business partnership that lasted for many years. Flagler, who was also the founder of Standard Oil's Florida East Coast Railway, was instrumental in opening Florida up as a vacation spot for the wealthy. Flagler is a man that Rockefeller was thinking of when he stated, "A friendship based on business is superior to a friendship based on friendship."

Flagler

Jay Gould has been a crucial part of Rockefeller's fortune. Because being in the oil trade meant nothing without a means to transport the oil, it is hard to believe that

Rockefeller would have made it without Jay Gould. Rockefeller, Flagler and others tried to make Cleveland as accessible as possible by three railroad lines and the Erie Canal. Gould was the one who bought the Erie Railroad, which he had previously purchased from Commodore Vanderbilt. Gould made an under-the table deal with Rockefeller & Flagler. They were in danger of losing all of their oil business and arranged a deal that allowed them a 75% rebate on shipping costs. Flagler's agreement with the Atlantic Railroad and Great Western Railroads made it impossible to compete with other refiners. Gould reported that his railroad delivered up to 60 oil cars per day. Rockefeller accepted any risk of injury or fire. Flagler or Rockefeller did not regret or be concerned by this strange deal. Rockefeller wasn't concerned about what people thought of his actions as he moved forward to amass greater wealth than anyone had ever seen.

Gould

Jay Gould was the one who arranged for Rockefeller's 1868 move to Euclid Avenue. It became Cleveland's famous "Millionaire's Row." The Rockefeller's house cost $40,000 which was quite a lot for the time, but it wasn't the most expensive in the area. Rockefeller wasn't known for showing off his wealth. He actually spent more time on the gardens that he and Cettie felt were unnecessary. Their lives were simple given their social status. They seldom socialized outside of going to the Symphony because of their opposition towards alcohol and what they considered to be the loose morals in the theater.

Bessie was the first child of four: Alice (who passed away shortly after her first birthday), Alta (1965), Edith (1966) and John Jr. (1967). Cettie Rockefeller believed in frugal living. Cettie more than John believed that their children would appreciate what was available to them if they were deprived of the things they could afford. John Jr. only wore dresses until he reached 8 years of age, because he was restricted to his sisters' old clothes. The Rockefeller children each had one bicycle. Despite John's assertions that it would be cheap to buy one each for them, they were mostly kept in the dark regarding their father's wealth. They were not granted money, they had to earn it. Sundays were reserved as time for prayer, church, and intensive Bible study. The family sang hymns every evening after dinner. They even prayed together each morning before breakfast. Children were also fined for lateness.

Author Rockefeller, Jr., and Author Rockefeller, Jr., 1915

Rockefeller had a strong relationship with his children, not unlike his father. Rockefeller installed a telegraph line at his home to allow him to communicate with his office. He would happily take care of a child who was crying, or get down on his knees for his children's play. Rockefeller was never one to gamble, drink or chase women. Rockefeller was home at nights and believed that his family would be better for it. Even if he was snoozing in a comfortable chair. Eliza, his mother and a regular visitor to his house, rotated among her children's houses. Devil Bill was kept informed about the lives of her grandchildren through letters that she passed on. He died suddenly, but she was able to accept him even though he was already married.

Rockefeller and Cleveland both became rich while they were still together. But, Rockefeller wasn't concerned about the volatile oil price. It was only used to lighten at the time, so there was no market like today. Flagler, Rockefeller and others realized that buying smaller refineries would bring stability to oil price. They felt that too much competition was a threat to the industry and that prices fluctuating too often could cause it to be damaged. To stabilize the oil industry, it was essential to consolidate its existing refineries. Rockefeller was, like many of his business choices, determined to do good for and not harm the oil industry.

Flagler had the idea to incorporate the business and then sell shares. On January 10, 1870 Rockefeller died along with Andrews. Flagler was the president of Standard Oil Company of Ohio. It was already America's biggest corporation at the time of its founding and controlled 10% national oil refineries. Standard Oil's title was not accidental, because Rockefeller wanted it imply consistency. Kerosene, a byproduct oil that has been used extensively as a fuel for lamps, is known to be unstable. Rockefeller wanted people to have faith in his product. He also wanted to set a price standard for the market.

Flagler and Rockefeller had no salary. Their only income was from the increase in their shares' value. Rockefeller felt this provided enough motivation to work. The Rockefeller name will be haunted for many years by the deal that Standard Oil's executive team made in January 1872. Rockefeller didn't care about Tom Scott who was the head of Pennsylvania Railroad but the idea of an exclusive agreement with Pennsylvania was attractive. Scott, known as South Improvement Company or SIC, arranged a contract that allowed Standard Oil to ship its product exclusively along the Pennsylvania, New York Central and Erie Railroads. The railroads affiliated with the SIC also received more business.

This deal was even more devastating for other oil company's because, while shipping costs were being increased, Standard Oil was actually getting shipping rebates. Standard Oil was also to receive a 40 cent per barrel rebate on every barrel of oil shipped from Standard Oil's non SIC rivals to Cleveland. This rebate was paid for by competitors. This was an unprecedented deal.

Ida Tarbell, a muckraking journalist, would be instrumental in the breaking up of Standard Oil. She was the granddaughter of a Pennsylvanian oilman. One word was all that could be found on each lips: "conspiracy 2". Rockefeller rebuffed it, and he still believed that rebates were part of normal business practices decades later. The deal was not yet illegal but it was certainly considered morally questionable. Rockefeller didn't invent the deal. Had he been more open about that, perhaps some of the public relations damage would have been avoided. It wasn't his way to explain his decisions.

Tarbell

Despite the morality, Standard Oil and its competition were reeling from the shock caused by the SIC contract. Standard Oil fought back, refusing to sell crude oil. The East Coast media spotted what the SIC was doing and voted for the independent oilmen. Rockefeller was then personally identified as the villain in an "Oil War" against the Pennsylvania oilmen. The charter for SIC was revoked April 1872 by Pennsylvania without any business transactions.

Rockefeller, however, ignored the criticism. His plan to take over oil companies was already in motion. He had already started the process to purchase nearly every Cleveland refinery. If he could see a refinery he wanted to buy, his first instinct was to use reason and flattery. Then he would appeal for brotherhood and how it would benefit the industry. John and William then tried different methods to persuade the owner of the refinery. John argued that it was profitable to "give the refinery owner a good sweating." This could be blackmailing, intimidation, or threats if necessary.

Rockefeller in 1872

Author Rockefeller never personally threatened anyone with harm. Standard Oil, however, had a network consisting of employees and spies that kept them informed about what the competitors were doing. Standard Oil would have a look at a refinery that was close to signing a deal. Rockefeller's spy would file an investigation and Rockefeller might make a better offer.

Standard Oil refinery in Cleveland from the late 19th-century

Rockefeller also used different tactics to control and expand the oil industry. Rockefeller orchestrated purchasing of materials required for the manufacture of oil barrels. He also bought all of those chemicals needed to refine it and dramatically cut the price of the product. All this was done in order to drive out his competitors. He was so concerned that the competition would find out what he was doing, the company started to communicate using code. Rockefeller even created his own codename, Chowder. One employee who quit due to disagreements about the company's business tactics said that "Results were exactly what the master required." He does not need to know the details."[3]

Standard Oil bought 22 out of 26 Cleveland-area oil refineries in a matter a mere weeks. This was what would be called the Cleveland

Massacre. Rockefeller turned 40 in October and Standard Oil bought 22 of the 26 oil refineries in Cleveland. Shortly thereafter, he would also take control of most oil wells as the marketing of oil.

Rockefeller was having difficulty managing Standard Oil's different divisions in 1882. He wanted to combine his interests but was prevented by a law that would not allow him to combine businesses with operations in different states. The solution was a trust. In 1882, Standard Oil Trust was established. This trust was to act as the corporation leading in the field of corporate business. A Board of Trustees formed and each stockholder received 20 Trust Certificates for every Standard Oil share. Rockefeller, who was head of the Trust, owned 9,000 shares. The Trust's estimated value was about $70 million. But, Standard was eventually sued by Ohio and the Trust dissolution was completed in 1892.

Standard Oil trust certificates

Ida Tarbell created a 19-part serial for McClure's magazine between 1902-1904. This represented a new form of journalism. Muckrakers sought to expose injustices, including racism, child labor, poverty, and racism. But McClure was McClure's target. She interviewed Rockefellers enemies, including Frank. Then she painted a portrait a man bent on becoming rich no matter how much it cost. Rockefeller didn't have much to defend because a lot of Tarbell's statements about Standard Oil were accurate.

Rockefeller shown as an industrial ruler in a 1901 cartoon

This was also during an era when President Donald Trump had made it clear he would pursue illegal trusts. Standard Oil was also on the Federal Government's radar after Tarbell's report. The Department of Justice sued Standard Oil in 1909 alleging it was an illegal monopoly and that Standard Oil had broken the 1890 Sherman Antitrust Act.

"Rebates to railroad companies for the combination; preference and restraint on the control of pipeline lines and unfair competition against them; contracts with rivals in restraints of trade; unfair competition methods such as local price cutting where necessary; espionage and operation of bogus independently owned companies and payment or rebates for oil with similar intent.

"The investigation revealed a number of flagrant discriminations committed by railroads for Standard Oil Co. and its related corporations. There have been very few exceptions to this rule, most notably from large California-based concerns. However, the Standard has been solely the beneficiary of discriminations like these. It has been proven that the company has unfair advantages over its competition in nearly all parts of the country. Some discriminations are so severe that they affect entire areas.

"Almost everywhere, the rates for shipping from the only or almost exclusive use of the Standard is lower than that from its competitors. Standard Oil Co. rates have been reduced to make it easier to get to markets. However, its competitors have kept them out of these markets by raising their rates. Trifling distance differences are excused by large rates favorable to Standard Oil Co.; however, large distance differences are ignored against the Standard. Sometimes connect roads prorate on oil, that is make through rates that are lower than the combination rate of local rates. At other times they refuse to prorate. Either way, their policy favors Standard Oil Co. Different methods may be used in different locations or under different conditions. The net result is that there is an open rate arrangement on petroleum oil from Maine to California which gives the Standard an unreasonable advantage over its competition.

"The evidence is conclusive that Standard Oil Co. charges excessively for its products where there is no other competition, and in particular where there are few chances of competition entering the area, and that it also cuts prices to a degree that leaves Standard little to no profit. The Standard's profit margin is even lower than that of the competitors, whose costs usually tend to be slightly higher."

A cartoon showing President Roosevelt as the baby Hercules against the serpents of Standard Oil

Rockefeller appeared in 1911 as president of the company. Standard Oil was then declared an illegal monopoly and was split into 37 companies on May 15, 2011. Rockefeller went on to be even wealthier because all of the pieces were more valuable than the whole. Author Rockefeller became America's second billionaire when Standard Oil was dismantled.

Chapter 5: Domestic Problems Follow John from New York

Rockefeller - "The only question regarding wealth is what you do with it."

Rockefeller, his family and friends had moved to New York City after it became impossible to manage offices at both New York City's Cleveland office. Standard Oil headquarters could be found at 26 Broadway. It is a famous building that was often just called its address. Rockefeller and the family lived in hotels when they arrived. But by 1884 their brownstone mansion was completed at 4 West 54th Street. Cettie and her family made it their winter-spring home. Cettie returned to Cleveland in early autumn. The family began to have more fun with their money and made more trips to Europe, even after the move. John, Jr., as an adult, remembered how his father couldn't understand Italian restaurant bills, in order to make sure he didn't owe any more, even when he was on vacation.

Rockefeller was enjoying his fortune. However, Devil Bill was back on his wanderings and continued his charade of being a medical healer. John and William had occasional contact, but Frank, his father who came to Kansas to hunt, was closer to him. John though was concerned that John's father might be a bigamist. He tried his best to keep the truth secret.

Eliza Rockefeller suffered an uncontrollable stroke in March 1889. She was left paralysed and she remained in William's Fifth Avenue mansion as her health declined. The sons of Eliza Rockefeller stayed at her bedside till she died, aged 76. She never realized that her husband was a bigamist.

Frank informed John of his father's asthma symptoms and advised him not to attend the Cleveland funeral for Eliza. John told Frank the reverend that Eliza had died. John refused to let Eliza's death certificate state that she was a widow. John maintained his insistence on Bill seeing his wife. John was furious for weeks after Bill didn't appear. Six months after Eliza's suicide, Bill finally showed in Cleveland. John was once again infuriated by his sight. He had originally paid in 1881 for his father's Park River Ranch, North Dakota, with the condition that Margaret Allen would never be taken there. But now he was so angry at his father that his father sold the ranch.

John and Bill had a fraught relationship, which lasted until Bill died. But, as Rockefeller grew wealthier and more prominent, the media became more curious about Rockefeller. A national manhunt was launched for his father in 1908 by Charles Johnston's surrogate son, and former con partner of Bill. Johnston has always been told that Devil Bill kept his affair with John Rockefeller a secret in order to avoid him embarrassment. It was also likely to prevent himself from being sued for his bigamy. Devil Bill Rockefeller, at the age 96, died in

1906. He was buried by his family in Freeport. William Levingston is the name of his tombstone.

Chapter 6: Rockefeller, Philanthropist

Rockefeller.

"I believe the ability and gift to make money comes from God. Like the instincts for literature, art, and music, mine must be developed to benefit the greater good of mankind. I believe that my gift has been given to me and I must use it for the good and welfare of others. Author Rockefeller

Rockefeller, who was in the midst of the dissolution of the Standard Oil Trust, began to crumble under the weight of his wealth and not knowing what to do. He was often overwhelmed by letters asking for money and people just standing in line outside 26 Broadway asking for loans. Cettie was always very careful about the causes they donated to, and he worried that he would give in to temptations. He wanted to be careful with charitable spending, just like he was with personal purchases.

Rockefeller was very conscious of his health. Unlike many industrial tycoons of Gilded Age, he did not overindulge in food. He believed in exercising outdoors, which included playing a lot of golf. He loved to take naps each day and believed herbal remedies could be effective, but the stress and pressure of work and charity became too much. He developed an autoimmune disease called alopecia in 1886. All his hair, including his trademark mustache and eyebrows, fell out. The photos of him show a hairless and stoic man that looked as though he had been 20 years old. For someone who had always been younger than he was, it was a remarkable change. In fact, by 1901, he was completely hairless. In fact, Charles Schwab sat beside him at a business dinner for the first time. Charles didn't even recognize him, and asked for his introduction.

Rockefeller, in March 1891, reached out to Frederick T. Gates to get help. He said that he couldn't simply give away money unless he investigated the cause properly, and that it was taking longer to investigate these causes than it took for Standard Oil to run. Rockefeller realized he could not abandon philanthropy. It was God's expectation that he would be a steward God's funds. Rockefeller also shared Andrew Carnegie's view that it was the duty to the wealthy to assist the needy. Carnegie had made his fortune through steel. His own funds were mostly used for libraries and schools. Rockefeller saw this admiration and sent him a letter in 1896 when the Carnegie Library in Pittsburgh was opened. Rockefeller wrote: "I would like that more men had the same attitude about money as you do; but rest assured, your example is going to bear fruits. The time will come when people of wealth will be more open to using it for the benefit others."

Frederick T. Gates agreed to Rockefeller's invitation to join him and manage his philanthropic operations. Gates was a Baptist minister. His inner turmoil was known to him from his encounters with doctors who told him they felt in no position to heal the sick. After his experience as a Baptist minister, Gates began to doubt the value and efficacy of medicine. Within a few years, he encouraged Rockefeller for money to be donated towards the establishment of a medical institution. Rockefeller hesitated to make this suggestion because he believed strongly in homeopathy. But John, Jr., who was 3 years old when John, Jr. died in 1901 from scarlet-fever, convinced Rockefeller to donate money for the medical sector. Rockefeller funded the Rockefeller Institute for Medical Research.

Gates

If there was a common theme to all of these stories, it was that Rockefeller funds were used to provide long-term assistance, not short-term relief. This was the philosophy of many industrial giants during the Gilded Era.

A lot of groundbreaking research was done using Rockefeller Foundation funding. Rockefeller's main concern was education. Rockefeller was also a major donor to Booker T. Washington's Tuskegee Institute. His Foundation has provided many grants. Many recipients include Albert Einstein as well as Ralph Ellison, the writer, and Bill T. Jones, the award-winning choreographer. In the 1930s the Foundation supported refugees fleeing Nazi persecution by placing them at New School, New York.

Chapter 7: Retirement, Rockefeller's Last Years, and His Legacy

A 1917 portrait featuring Rockefeller

"I was raised to play and work early in life.

My life has been a long and happy vacation.

A mix of work and play.

I stopped worrying about it along the road.

And God was gracious to me each day." - Author Rockefeller

Rockefeller's own illness led him to believe that he could not maintain the pace of his work, which was fitting. He took eight month off in 1891, at the request of his family. Standard Oil was not something he thought about or invested much time thinking about. He spent his days at his Cleveland home riding his bike, tending the farm with the hired workers, and he even joked that his singing was also a hobby. He gained 15 pounds by the end Cleveland summer. He also had a healthier complexion and more energy.

Gates was assured that Rockefeller did not need additional money and that he had everything he needed. Standard Oil dividends paid him $3 million per annum without him having to lift a single finger. He was also worried that working hard would make it worse. He thought of retiring, but it wouldn't be until 1897 that the real freedom from daily work came to him, even though he was slowly being less seen on 26 Broadway.

Rockefeller took his retirement quietly. There was no formal ceremony, no goodbye luncheon or dinner. Because of the numerous lawsuits targeting Standard Oil, he was still president of the company. But, he was president only in name. Because of his fame, and all the publicity, people didn't realize that he was just a figurehead. John Jr., his son, assumed control of Standard Oil. Junior was not quite as well-equipped as his father to deal with the pressure of leading Standard Oil. Junior, 36, retired in 1910. He devoted the remainder of his life and energy to philanthropy.

Kykuit (Dutch for "lookout") is what Junior Rockefeller was likely to feel when he started supervising the construction and maintenance of Kykuit. Tarbell's expose regarding Standard Oil led to a press siege of the family. The mansion with 40 rooms is located on the highest point Pocantico Hills. It spans 3,400 acres and boasts a spectacular view of Central Park. It was not finished until 1913. It remained a Rockefeller family getaway for four generations before it was included in the National Trust for Historic Preservation. Senior built a 18-hole golf course at the location in 1901. Senior was known for playing golf every day at 12 o'clock p.m. It was while he was on the course with a local priest that he found out Standard Oil had to be dissolved. He suggested to the priest to buy Standard Oil stock now.

Henry Ford was born just as Thomas Edison's lightbulb seemed to be hurting Standard Oil's need for kerosene. America's fascination with cars would grow and the need for gasoline would follow. Rockefeller even joined the fray by purchasing a car. Afternoon car rides were one of his greatest pleasures. He liked to see his driver attempt to beat the speed record from the previous day. He liked having attractive women around him. He would usually have one person on each side of himself in the backseat, with a blanket pulled up over their heads to provide comfort and shield them from prying eyes.

Rockefeller's retirement was just as pleasant as it sounds. Rockefeller became more genial, and even wore hair wigs to cover the baldness of his head at social functions. He thoroughly enjoyed spending time at his grandchildren, especially Junior's son

Nelson, who would eventually become vice-president of the Gerald Ford government.

Nelson in 1954

Junior was more troubled by the lofty expectations associated with being a Rockefeller father than his dad was. He was susceptible to nervous breakdowns and believed the entire world was watching his family. Junior was a strict father. He allowed no room for error and was fearful of spoiling his children. Abby, his wife, rebelled at the idea and insist that she wasn't going. Abby Rockefeller, their mother, was much more approachable to their children. She was also the voice in reason when Junior was difficult to manage.

Junior felt more guilty than his father for any business dealings. He once noted that he never asked for money and that it never brought him joy. Junior was also irritated by the portrayal a father as a bad guy, so he worked to save the family's name.

Rockefeller maintained that his goal to live to 100 was his ultimate goal, and he lived to the fullest extent of his siblings' lives. Frank, who did not reconcile with his brother due to business disagreements, passed away in April 1917. Frank was so determined to hold his grudge against his relatives that he purchased a separate plot in Cleveland's Lake View Cemetery. John and William attended Frank's funeral service. There was no animosity with Frank's spouse or children. Any debts Frank owed in his brothers' names were promptly cancelled. William passed away from pneumonia due to throat cancer in 1922. His fortune was worth more than $200 million, but it mostly went towards his children. John felt no obligation to donate his earnings.

Rockefeller explained to reporters, on his 80th birthday, that he attributed his long-term success to daily golfing and a tablespoonfull of olive oil. Even as Rockefeller grew older, he never lost his zest and enthusiasm for life. Rockefeller, as always, was not interested in dwelling on the difficulties of life. He preferred to spend his time with his family and friends, which he did. Rockefeller became known for entertaining young women after Cettie passed away. Rockefeller loved to flirt with and tease his female guests, even at golf. Ira Warner, who was a widower and lived in Connecticut, was frequented at Kykuit. She also visited the Casements in Ormond, Florida, which is his winter home.

Rockefeller seems to be more sane and more playful in his 80s or 90s than when he was a child. He liked stylish clothes, and escorted women along to concerts, dances, and the opera. He also enjoyed movies with lovely blonde leads. Junior was more interested in movies featuring beautiful, blonde women than Rockefeller. Junior didn't keep up with the trends of 1920s fashion and, despite Senior's requests that he relaxes, Junior was so overwhelmed by his responsibilities that Junior developed a variety of ailments including exhaustion, headaches, temporary deafness, and fatigue. Junior was advised to be vegetarian and to reduce the amount of work he did after he checked himself into the Battle Creek Sanitarium. He was told that he had to work less but play more. However, it was too much for him. He was plagued by headaches almost every single day. He felt stressed out because his father kept giving him more money than he could afford (his father once gave him more that half a billion dollars).

Senior carried on his cheerful life. He held a Christmas Party at Casements every Christmas for all of his neighbors. Rockefeller would come to the door in a tailored suit and greet everyone, before handing out gifts. After that, he was the one leading the neighborhood children through Christmas carols. He was friendly and open to strangers. His photograph was taken.

After a lifetime of hiding from the press, he voluntarily allowed himself to be photographed on his 90th birthday. He was dressed in an elegant suit and took a few shots on the fairway. This provided an alternative view of a man many Americans consider a corrupt tycoon.

Rockefeller reached 97 and was no longer able or able enough to go church. So he began listening to sermons on radio. He never spoke of death but he certainly thought about it. Henry Ford was told by him that he would meet him in Heaven. Ford replied, "You will if I get in."[6] He had been aging and was becoming weaker. This is why it was perhaps a surprise when he died on May 23, 1927 from a heart attack. He didn't reach his goal, which was to be 100.

The legacy left by Author Rockefeller is complicated. Many would have laughed if they had told them that the Rockefeller surname would be associated to philanthropy. Standard Oil's business methods were brutal, ruthless in today's terms and patently illegal. However, historians as well as biographers have refuted the idea that Rockefeller had been immoral or a criminal baron. Alan Nevins, a 20th-century American historian, wrote that "The rise and fall of Standard Oil men to great prosperity was not because of poverty." It was not meteor-like. However, it took over 25 years to achieve this feat by bravely venturing into a dangerous field that few large capitalists would consider. This was done through arduous labors as well as more sagaciously and farsighted planning that had ever been used in any American industry. The oil fortunes in 1894 were no more than the steel fortunes and banking fortunes. However, it is the assertion by Standard magnates that they derived their wealth from the appropriation of 'the properties of others' that most challenges us. We have plenty of evidence that Rockefeller consistently offered fair terms for competitors and bought them out, either in stock, cash or both, at fair assessments. An impartial historian also stated that Rockefeller was significantly more humane to his competitors than Carnegie. The conclusion of another historian is that Rockefeller's wealth was "the least tainted" of all the great riches of his time.

Rockefeller's fortune provided seed money that has enabled him to do many good deeds. Rockefeller acted as he did when running his business. He trusted the people who would use the funds and did not limit how they could be used. Rockefeller gave $35 million to the Rockefeller Foundation as the president in 1913. He also gave $65,000,000 in the next year.

Although the Rockefeller Foundation has been surpassed in its giving capacity by the Bill and Melinda Gates Foundation many years ago, its total endowment still exceeds $3 billion and it remains one of the largest foundations in the United States. Rockefeller's famous quote was "I've tried turning every disaster into a chance." The man who began with $40 in Cleveland business school could have left a different legacy. While Standard Oil and its history will remain the starting point for his legacy, Rockefeller changed the destination. Rockefeller merely wanted to promote "the well-being of mankind throughout the world", and there is no question that Rockefeller's money has done that.

Father of Future Billionaires

Success is about doing the uncommon things well.

-- John D. Rockefeller

William Rockefeller is the great grandfather of five brothers, who are currently the head of the family. John D. Rockefeller is the father. He was a vulgar horsethief as well as a petty criminal.

Sources state that Eliza Davison, a wealthy farmer's daughter, became Mrs. Rockefeller due to her "secular posture" and abstinence of wine (drunkenness is one of few vices William Rockefeller could be free from).

The parents refused to marry this girl, as the father of the girl was a notorious card player and kidnapper who had earned a bad reputation.

Officially William Rockefeller was selling medicines. However, he was not a normal pharmacist. He did not have an education. He also sold charlatan medication, cooperating with various healers and mystifiers.

William traveled to the northeastern United States and sold worthless medical potions. He was either a "botanical practitioner," a "famous cancer specialist", or an impoverished deaf-blind person.

John Rockefeller (the son of William) was 10 years when his family needed to move. It was almost an escape. As evidenced by those time documents, the reason for moving was quite interesting: William Rockefeller was arrested as a horsethief.

William appeared in Richford alone, without the family. A handsome man, with a light brown beard and new coat, William was an unusual sight in Richford. - Carefully ironed trousers. On his chest was the sign, "I am both deaf" William, nicknamed Big Bill and quickly learned everything about everyone.

Eliza Davison was captivated by his lush beard. She exclaimed "

"I would marry the man I saw if he were not dumb and deaf!"

The "cripple", who was standing in the background, recognized that there was plenty of work to be done.

Bill's ears were just as accurate as the radars of the time, so he gave Eliza five-thousand dollars as adowry. They were soon married, and John Rockefeller arrived in the light after two years.

God blessed William with incredible charisma. Eliza did no break up with her husband, even though she was aware that her fiance could understand everything. Even when her husband brought Nancy Brown, Nancy's mistress, to the house to get married, she didn't leave him. Eliza gave birth to William and Eliza.

William went to work in the evening. Eliza woke to the sound a pebble hitting the window.

She ran outside the house, tore back the bolt and opened the gate. Her husband arrived in the yard, on a horse, in a fresh suit and sometimes with diamonds. He made a lot of money. Bill was the name of his neighbor; some called him Bill, while others considered him a professional gangster.

However, the family could not settle in a new home. Under cover of darkness, they fled because of a new scandal. After several years of wandering, Rockefeller family settled in Cleveland.

He was just 17 years old when he married Margaret.

William Rockefeller had a close to fifty-year-long second marriage. Margaret Levingston found out that her husband was one of the most wealthy men in the world during his last years.

Young Rockefeller

Success is about doing the uncommonly good things.

-- John D. Rockefeller

John Rockefeller (7 years old) begged his mom for the blue porcelain dish on the fireplace's mantle. He then began to put the coppers he had collected for candy and entertainment in it. His peers bought sweets to ride the carousel. But, pale Johnny was not interested in the others and could look at his wealth for hours.

In his memoirs, the author recalls:

"One my first experiences was working for a neighbor to harvest potatoes for several days. He was a successful farmer and very entrepreneurial. I was probably around 12 at the moment. Every day, the farmer gave us coins.

I had been saving these tiny amounts in a bank piggy bank but quickly realized that the money I could make by digging potatoes 100 times a week, I could also get without squeezing my fingers if $ 50 was in the bank. This discovery led me think it would be beneficial to have money to pay my slave and vice-versa.

William prospered and Eliza was able to support her family. She was not certain if her husband will return and so she continued to farm the land, saving every penny.

Half-starved, half-clothed in old clothes and running to school, her sons went to work after school. William lived in shame and struggled to make ends meet at home.

Rockefeller made his fortune. He got into logging, bought 100 acres of land, built a smokehouse and expanded the house. Little John, a passionate lover of music, reading, and church services, looked up at his father. It was a quiet boy who was always contemplative.

John looked absent-minded. It seemed as though John was always working to solve an intractable issue. This was deceiving. John had a sharp memory and was very calm. He was a keen player of checkers. He spent much time thinking over each move and never lost.

John Rockefeller had extremely dry skin. He didn't have a boyish look in his eyes. He lived a hard life. Profits were his only passion.

One of his three sisters observed that "If oatmeal fell from the sky Johnny would be the one to run for the plate."

Seven-yearold Johnny had raised turkeys on his own and sold them immediately for fifty dollars to a neighbor farmer. He borrowed the money from his neighbor to make seven percent per annum. He did not play any of the typical childhood games.

John was a practical youngster. He was able and willing to help others, even those who were less fortunate than him. John discovered that his grandfather was friendly, talkative, and weak.

His mother was dedicated to hard work, loyalty to duty, and a strong will. John worked every day from dawn till the first stars of the universe, and only took a few days off to rest. William Rockefeller, the brilliant schemer, had a gentle but almost sensual affection for money. He liked to leave banknotes at his desk and to put his hands into them. This passion was passed to his son.

John Rockefeller never became a libertine and a bigamist. Although he was not accused of rape as his father, Rockefeller learned a lot by his father.

From his earliest years of childhood, he was actively involved in business. His first business venture was to buy a pound and then divide it into smaller groups. The future billionaire kept the money safe in a piggybank. Soon he began to lend money at a fair percentage to his father.

John was generally viewed as being insensitive, greedy, and arrogant. He knew how best to hide his feelings. He was still sensitive. John ran to his backyard to help his sister who had died. He fell to the ground, and he stayed there all day.

Rockefeller never became the monster that he portrays as a child. Rockefeller asked his former classmate about his love and, after finding out that she was now widowed and in poverty, decided to award her a monthly pension.

It's hard not to determine the type of John Rockefeller. All thoughts, emotions, and desires subordinated to Rockefeller's great goal -- to get wealthy.

He was transformed into a business engine, which allowed him to create business ideas and exploit his subordinates. John would either succumb to exhaustion or prosper.

Rockefeller's success as a businessman and wealthy man shows that he had extraordinary intuition.

John was in high school when his father cheated creditors. His father then left the family and seduced a second servant.

William Rockefeller married another lady, changed his name, and went underground from his wife and sons. John did his father's death in the middle of the night, and his family will not see him again.

John Rockefeller had a close friendship with Mark Hanna, who was also a student of John Rockefeller. Hanna would later start the company that is today the largest in the northwest United States.

Hanna was resourceful and resourceful. But even Hanna was affected by the young Rockefeller's monetary fanaticism. Hanna later said about her childhood friend: "John was clearly obsessed with money in those years.

John Rockefeller said that he could not work for four thousand dollars the first time he was paid as a cashier in a trade firm. He stood at his desk for five minutes and opened the safe.

Career

I can't think of anything more pathetic and despicable than a man who works all day for money.

-- John D. Rockefeller

He is 16 years-old and is moving to Cleveland. John D. Rockefeller wants to be an accountant.

It is unbearably hot. However, a young male in a black suit and dark tie persistently walks from one office the other. He does NOT want to go back home to the Rockefeller Farm. Hewitt & Tuttle appoints him as their assistant accountant.

The fact that his first salary was only after four months was not of any importance. He was allowed into the glittering world of business and he marched bravely towards the much-coveted hundred thousand. John Rockefeller behaved almost like a lover.

He ran screaming in a fit and passion to a work colleague. "I am doomed!"

The poor fellow was unable to resist the urge to shout, and he eventually gave up. Rockefeller refused to drink, not even coffee. He also did not smoke, attend dance classes or go to the theater. He was delighted to receive a check for $4000.

He was called by girls looking for dates. The young clerk told them that he could meet only at church. He believed he had been chosen by God and that the temptations of the flesh didn't bother him.

Rockefeller knew the God blesses good people and made it his daily routine to work until late at night. God granted him what was best for him.

Rockefeller was very fortunate. The Union declared its withdrawal and the Civil War began. Federal government needed hundreds upon thousands of uniforms or rifles, millions on cartridges, mountains of dried food, tobacco, and biscuits.

The golden age of speculation started, and Rockefeller was co-owner at a brokerage with a start capital of four thousand dollar. He made good fortune.

He found a gold mine. In all the houses, from those of the Vanderbilts or Carnegies to those of Chinese immigrants, kerosene lamps had been lit.

Maurice Clark, Rockefeller's partner in business, said that John believed only two things on this earth: Baptist dogma (and oil).

He dreamed of oil fields gushing from the ground in the night. The gloomy man in black walked around the office singing and hugging secretaries after he had made a good deal.

John started his career in 1855 at the tender age of 16 as an accounting clerk at a Cleveland-based trading firm. He was at draft age when the Civil War brokeout in the United States. The $300 payment was for military service. This was a common practice for those in the North who had funds.

Rockefeller met Maurice B. Clark soon after, a novice entrepreneur. Clark suggested Rockefeller open his own company that sells grain, meat, and other products. John left his business as a trader to open Clark and Rockefeller. The partnership was a small grocery shop typical of the era. The idea was very well received by the new settlers that arrived in the region. Clark demanded $2000 to start the business. Rockefeller, however, had only $900. But Clark, an aspiring businessman, knew where to find more money. William Rockefeller promised his children $1,000 each when they turned 21. John was 20 years of age when he entered into a contract. William would provide John with $1,000 and also earn interest. William Rockefeller taught his kids that kinship wasn't a hindrance for business.

He was willing to make various deals with relatives.

After receiving the funds, John opened Clark and Rockefeller. However, these young entrepreneurs proved to be destined for success. The entire year was spent processing transactions worth nearly half a mile and earning approximately $ 4,400. Maurice Clark remembers that Rockefeller worked hard and managed all aspects of the company. He communicated with bankers and they were amazed by his knowledge and accuracy. John also approached clients directly. And the opposite happened: The partners were responsible for everything up to the penny.

On Saturdays he would work in the office cursing at a partner, who called him up to the lake to fish. Rockefeller was still a grocer five years later and had invested four thousand in a young, fast growing Cleveland oil refinery. The oil business was regarded as the industrial equivalent for the Wild West back in 1863.

In the 1960s, Pennsylvania Railroad attempted dominance of crude oil transportation. They did so to support New York and Philadelphia's interests. Many Cleveland refiners panicked fearing their access to raw material would be restricted.

Rockefeller, on one hand, made the most of the situation by negotiating agreements with two railroads, Jay Gould's Erie Railroad (New York Central's Lake Shore) and Jay Gould's Erie Railroad (Jay Gould's Erie Railroad). Henry Flagler and Rockefeller agreed to receive secret discount of 30-75% on officially published railway tariffs. They also received regular cargo.

With this predictable and sustainable business, carriers could achieve significant increases in their labor productivity. Pennsylvania Railway no longer posed a threat as a transport company.

Rockefeller, the world's most important refiner, could not ship sufficient volumes to qualify for concessions in railway tariffs.

Then he began to coordinate deliveries with other Cleveland-based oilmen. As high profits at low initial costs and high profits lured many more people into distilling oil, their tendency to replace competition was intensified.

By 1870, the volume of crude oil produced by distillation plants had tripled. Rockefeller estimates that 90% percent of processors lost their income as a result.

The Standard Oil Company

We must never forget that we are refining oils for the poor man. He must have it cheaply and good."

-- John D. Rockefeller

Colonel Edwin Drake discovered the first ever oil field in the United States, located in Titusville. American business gained what it didn't have: a dedicated army of young, experienced people that were eager to make their fortune after the Civil War.

John D. Rockefeller created his own company in Cleveland in 1870. Titusville (and the surrounding towns) were literally bursting over with crude oil at that time. They were also teeming in people trying to make their money off it. Numerous drilling rigs were provided and nearly all of them were operated in different ways by different companies.

The pipeline runs through hundreds of distilleries, which are almost useless without oil distillation.

Rockefeller's Standard Oil Company in Cleveland was only one of 26 companies that were struggling to survive on a fragile market with just one supplier.

The price of crude oils ranged from $13 to 10 cents per barrel in the 1860s. Rockefeller saw the economic potential that a new industry offered and was the first one to take notice. The resulting product, kerosene, could heat homes and shine light on the streets of cities in rapid growth.

From a business viewpoint, oil was not even a significant part of oil refining. It was extracted directly from the same field. The oil was identical in all its physical characteristics. So, "black money" has always been the same.

All cleaning methods were the exact same. It is possible to use crude oil in industry by removing impurities. There was no added-value component that would affect the prices of different finished products. Transport is what made the difference in value.

The margin of the company's ability to play was greater if it was cheaper for the driver to transport oil from field to refinery and factory to market. Conversely, profit margins would be smaller if transportation was more expensive.

John D. Rockefeller had a very analytical and religious nature. Such formulas were actually like scripture. You can solve the transport problem and then put order to the most chaotic free market in America. Without them, oil would continue to be an unacceptablely unstable industry.

The oil business was in disarray, and the situation was worsening every day. Someone had the courage to stand firm.

It has become a way of life for the adventurous Rockefeller. It was necessary to solve transport problems. This will allow you to defeat your competition and dictate the terms of play.

Rockefeller was successful in resolving the transportation issue. Rockefeller entered the South Improvement Company as a member of shippers/carriers. At the start of 1872, Rockefeller made an agreement with three railway companies (Pennsylvania Central & Erie) for the lion's part of all oil transportation.

Standard Oil Company was able to receive preferential railroad tariffs in return. In contrast, its competitors in oil refining were subject to high punitive price increases. Rockefeller obtained detailed information about South Improvement Company's shipments which was invaluable in helping him reduce their prices.

Although the secret agreement was kept from all parties, it became known. After the information got out, torch-wielding mobs took to streets in Titusville. Franklin, Oil City, Oil City, and other oil producing cities. They destroyed railroad tracks and attacked Standard Oil cars. Within two months, Rockefeller's secret deal was declared illegal by the courts.

But he was already enjoying great success. Standard Oil Company quickly acquired 22 of its 26 competitors' businesses in just six weeks. This brutal operation became known as "The Cleveland Massacre".

Vendors realized that Rockefeller was a huge transport cost-savings advantage and they would still be in financial ruin. They therefore agreed to sell. Standard Oil Company became the nation's largest oil refining centre by taking over Cleveland's entire oil business in 1872.

Rockefeller became disillusioned with the volatility of this industry which had a negative impact on profitability. He needed a plan.

His proposal to reduce oil production by voluntary restriction was rejected in Pittsburgh. Rockefeller was then able to manage fluctuations in the prices of crude oil used for refining. Rockefeller disapproved when the oil producers refused to compromise on stabilizing prices.

The Company Gained Momentum

"It is wrong that people of great wealth assume that they are always happy,"

-- John D. Rockefeller

John Rockefeller decided that the only solution was to take over the national refining plant.

The Standard Oil Company's "fee" was immediately paid and other Cleveland acquisitions soon followed. The Great Depression which followed the panic at the stock market on September 18,1873 helped tremendously. Standard Oil Company started to buy rivals outside of Cleveland.

Rockefeller had a unique method. He gave enterprise managers the opportunity to read his books. It's all there.

When they saw that his production was very efficient and that he could offer products at lower prices while still making a profit, the two stopped resisting a merger. Standard Oil Company, Ohio, USA, was not allowed to have assets other than its home state under the terms of registration.

John D. Rockefeller refused to be stopped. He ordered the companies to continue their work under the old names and not make any written references to the merger.

Rockefeller won control of the major refineries in Philadelphia, and Pittsburgh in secret meetings in 1874. The new allies of Rockefeller began to purchase local competitors. Within two decades, the number Pittsburgh processors fell from 22 to just one.

Standard Oil Company gained greater control over major oil refining centers in New York, West Virginia, Baltimore and other areas near Pennsylvania.

Standard Oil Company was almost 90 per cent of the United States' crude oil production in 1877.

Rockefeller bought 53 refineries. 32 were shut down, leaving the most efficient. As a result, assets of the company increased even further. Standard Oil Company managed to reduce the cost for refining oil by three-quarters thanks to the increased volume. The company's revenues grew quickly and its market share rose rapidly.

Rockefeller once declared to a Cleveland rival: "I have means to create wealth that you even couldn't imagine!"

John D. Rockefeller has added cruelty to the basic attributes inherited by his father - intrigue and cunning - He once stated categorically to his wife: "A person who succeeds at life must sometimes go against it." And every day, he was a living proof of this principle in his business operations. He said, "You may not be scared that your hand might be cut off," but your body will suffer.

Rockefeller made falsified transactions when threats failed. He bought people, or at most their voices, if that did not work. He also bought support from the press.

Ohio senator got a $44,000 "lobbying payment" for discrediting state attorney general, who had allegedly interfered with Standard Oil Company. This was a fairly common practice, according the Rockefeller Reports.

Rockefeller was able to control ten percentage of the national refinery industry during the 1872'massacre. Standard Oil Company owned more than 90 percent of all the oil in the world, and John D. Rockefeller rapidly became wealthy. But there were still two variables that the company couldn't control. It was necessary to transport the oil from someplace in order to purify it. To have any economic value, it must also be sold.

Rockefeller would be unable to dominate the end of the process and maximize profits as long as he didn't have complete control. It was now that he could expand his reach.

The company took delivery assurance into consideration and went through every step of the production process, from producing tanks, railway cars, and pipelines to its own exploration, and oil production.

Standard Oil Company has increased its monopoly status by investing heavily in oil transportation. Railways, fearful of the forecasts of geologists concerning the rapid depletion national oil fields, and the enormous costs associated with increasing traffic, did not rush to act.

Rockefeller completed the modernization at New Jersey's Weehawken railroad terminal.

Standard Oil Company received preferred tariffs and valuable information regarding the cargoes other processors. This secured the right to prevent the transportation of competitors' oil. The company started its own fleet when the railways refused funding the new tanks which would replace the oil barrels.

Rockefeller also enjoyed an edge over the market's weaker participants. Standard Oil eventually bought a stake at another pipeline company, and its network became increasingly important in oil business.

Soon, the Rockefeller pipe companies and their obvious competition formed a cartel for increased production and fixing prices.

Standard Oil Company took control of distribution and sales to stabilize the supply chain. Oil was typically sold on a market by independent intermediaries which could sometimes cut as much a five-cents off a gallon worth of kerosene.

Rockefeller felt this was an unacceptable loss and a poor way to control and grow sales.

Rockefeller would have Rockefeller say later that "we had the to develop methods for sales much better then those that existed back then." "We had the ability to sell two,, three, or more gallons of oil in places where one was sold before. The available distribution channels were not sufficient."

Rockefeller began by discrediting independent operators, and replaced them using his own delivery- and sales services. This allowed him to have enough control over the industry. His employees delivered oil to national markets and department stores in specially-built vans.

Vans could even sell oil in bulk to areas where the population density is high. This broke the line between wholesale oil and retail oil trade, further confirming the belief all oil was from Standard Oil Company.

The company owned almost all American oil distillation. By the end 19th century, it also controlled the nation's second-largest iron mill. It also operated thousands of railroad cars, barges, and ships. It also had a presence in the iron and steel industries.

The vertical integration of the company was completed by the 1890s.

Rockefellers Fight

I have many ways to make my money, that you do not know.

-- John D. Rockefeller

Oil had flowed from Standard Oil Company's well, passed through Standard Oil Company's pipeline, and was finally cleaned at Standard Oil Company Refinery. Finally, it was shipped to tanks where it was stored until being sold to the final consumer by Standard Oil Company agents.

Standard Oil Company did not depend on incompetent suppliers, uncooperative distributors, or any other problems in the market to continue its operations.

Rockefeller achieved order. He was probably assisted by his 12 golden laws. Money started to flow from that moment.

Rockefeller accumulated the largest fortune over the next few years. Rockefeller earned nearly two dollars per second and more that 50 million dollars each year when Americans were content to earn just two dollars per day.

John D. Rockefeller didn't just devour his rivals and create a vertically connected corporation with a highly controlled product line, he was not the first. Trusts and monopolies were everywhere.

Rockefeller could do business more efficiently. He created his own modern management organization to manage the vast empire. He also relied upon advanced technology.

The telegraph, which was invented in 1885 by Standard Oil Company, was moved to a new corporate headquarters on 26

Broadway, Manhattan. It was a groundbreaking advancement in the national communications network.

Rockefeller could stay in contact with the entire Standard Oil Company, and be in touch with people at least once an hour. Micromanagement was the danger.

Rockefeller's genius did not give in to this temptation. Rockefeller didn't attempt to manage his empire solely by his own initiative or by cultivating fear.

Rockefeller managed Standard Oil Company by using committees. Production committee was in charge of the production while procurement committee handled the procurement. This approach is today a standard for any management system.

Rockefeller's committee system of defiance was created over 100 years ago for effective control of a disobedient and consolidated enterprise.

Historians claim that Rockefeller felt it was essential to be at the center of the table when he attended meetings of the executive board, where the title boss was the ultimate truth.

John D. also realized he had made a difference in the world. Alfred D. Chandler Jr. is a business historian who called Rockefeller, "a new subtype of economic men -- a salary manager."

Brookings Institution reveals that between 1880-1820, when Rockefeller achieved complete global dominance, the United States' number of professional managers increased six-fold. It went from 161,000 to almost a billion.

In response to growing demand for the profession in 1898, Chicago's and California's universities established a new direction within education: The Faculty of Business. New York University had business departments, while Dartmouth university also had them. Harvard University opened the Faculty of Business in 1908.

Rockefeller, at the end he lived, stated that Standard Oil Company had "become the ancestor of the whole economic administration system." She revolutionized the business world." While the tycoon may have been right, he decided to erase many of the less-than-stellar points from his past.

In a fascinating series of interviews, William Inglis from New York conducted with Rockefeller between 1917 and 1919, Rockefeller refuted nearly every accusation against Standard Oil Company, Ida Tarbell, and himself.

It is not known if these interviews were intended as publications -- they were broadcast 60-years after his death -- or whether they were simply used to relieve Rockefeller of his conscience and prepare Rockefeller for his meeting at the Creator.

In all cases, the interview stories back up the facts. Nelson Rockefeller asked John D. his grandfather to interview him about his thesis. John D. responded that he didn't want to.

Evidently, he couldn't lie to his grandson as he was born on exactly the same day.

Rockefeller was fond of pointing out that Rockefeller and his business were covered by the law after the fact. Although the "Cleveland Massacre", which was a secret railroad deal, was not illegal at the moment, the courts soon rejected such actions.

Only after the creation of an interstate commerce committee in 1887, were railway payments returned illegally. Trade restrictions that served to establish vertically integrated trusts continued to be legal until the passage of the Sherman Antitrust Act 1890.

Rockefeller's and Standard Oil Company's operations often went beyond the bounds of the law. In his correspondence, historians have discovered that Rockefeller bribed politicians to influence legislation while he was collecting material for his biography.

Rockefeller believed that McKinley was a necessary expense and therefore the 250 thousand dollars he spent in 1896 on it was the most innocent. The businessman's conduct was not affected either by the Sherman Antitrust Act, nor the Interstate Commerce Commission.

Rockefeller was more determined to bypass the legal obstacles faced by his company, and he found strong assistants not as interested in legal subtleties or ethics.

Henry Flagler as well as John D. Archibald. Ida Tarbell (American progressive journalist, Henry Demarest Lloyd) and Ida Tarbell (a writer, journaliste, researcher, biographer, and lecturer in the 19th century) gathered a large amount of evidence proving

Rockefeller's and Standard Oil Company's illegal and questionable actions.

In 1906, just one years after Ida Tarbell's McClures articles had been published, the magnate hired his initial publicist to improve their public image. Rockefeller perhaps underestimated at first the degree of hatred towards him and Roosevelt's great desire for him to become his political capital.

Rockefeller bought political figures easily and could not imagine a better way to handle them. He ignored the storm for most of his life, as he considered himself to be serving greater interests. Clearing up inefficiencies was a noble deed that benefited not only the economy but also God.

Roosevelt had resigned by that time, and the power was now transferred to William Howard Taft.

On May 15, 2011, having collected 23 volumes worth of testimony and over

12,000 pages in 21 years, and having convened 11 separate lawsuits with 444 witnesses each, the US Supreme Court ruled Standard Oil Company Trust to be a monopoly fragmentation.

Rockefeller learned the news on the course. His reaction was to inform his golf partners to invest in Standard Oil Company shares. John D.'s wisest advice was this. Standard Oil Company was splintered into 34 distinct companies. These included the parent corporations of modern industrial leaders such ExxonMobil (BP Amoco), Conoco and Chevron. Rockefeller kept control of each.

Rockefeller's business had an estimated cost of $ 300 Million in 1911 when the Supreme Court gathered for its last meeting.

Two years later, the "sentence" was executed by the federal Government. This "cost", now worth $900,000,000, rose to $900,000,000. It was the greatest success

Rockefeller ever experienced. At that time oil had a new purpose, the car.

John D. Rockefeller wasn't only richer due to the Supreme Court ruling, but it also didn't make him repent. In 1913 when approximately twenty thousand strikers were evicted from company-owned houses at the Rockefeller-controlled coal mine, the state police intervened, shot the strikers and set fire to a tent camp where they took refuge.

Dozens died from the fire including children and women. Rockefeller blamed the blood of his father and laid blame on strikers who "rashly", refused to give up their right union membership.

A million dollars in 1913 would be equivalent to 13 billion dollars today. The comparison of these figures, as biographers note, is not balanced.

The entire federal budget of 1913 was $715million. That's almost $200 million more than the net "costs" of Rockefeller. The federal debt in 1913 was approximately 1.2 Billion dollars. Three-quarters were paid off by Rockefeller.

Personal Life

"Do the right thing. But, it's not enough to do the right thing. People need to know that you are doing what is right."

-- John D. Rockefeller

He was twenty five years old, and his acquaintances believed that he would remain engaged to accounting forever. John Rockefeller did have a nine-year wait for his miracle, but -miracles do sometimes happen.

Laura Celestia Spelman grew up in a wealthy, well-respected home. She was an avid reader who also tried her hand as a literary editor and was able match Rockefeller in almost every respect. Laura was a Puritan. Theatre and dancing were her vices. And her soul rested with her church.

The future Mrs. Rockefeller preferred black to other colors. They met at school. He confessed his love to him, and she replied that he must first do something in life.

The story is quite sad but it wasn't. The boy who started out small was transformed into a tall, handsome, and fit young man. Laura (her mother's name was Settie), was a beautiful young woman. She was an excellent musician and took three hours daily piano lessons. Rockefeller was a master musician and Eliza was enraged by his household chores.

John D. Rockefeller wasn't able to freeze completely, but Laura knew that this was possible. Rockefeller paid $118 to get a diamond engagement ring. That was a great feat.

The wedding was modest. After the honeymoon Rockefeller, the house they lived in was rented at a very low rent. They didn't hire servants.

He owned the largest Cleveland oil refinery at this time. The bride's parents are wealthy and highly respected in Cleveland. There was no coverage of the wedding in the newspapers. He hated being talked about. Rockefeller's subordinates and colleagues feared him like fire, but his wife regarded him as the kindest man.

He was at Standard Oil Company each day at exactly 9:15 a.m., and it was rapidly becoming one the most prominent companies in the United States. He was tall with a pale and clean-shaven facial features. He wore a white silk hat, gloves and an umbrella on his head.

Rockefeller quietly greeted his subordinates. Then he inquired about the health of them and then quietly walked into his office. He did not raise his voice, didn't get nervous, and his face was always the same - it wasn't possible to disturb him. One day, a mad contractor rushed into the room and began screaming for half an hour. Rockefeller, furious and red-faced, sat behind the table and exhaled.

"Forgive me, please. I didn't catch what your were talking about." Could you repeat?

He always had lunch and then went to his office for a tour.

Rockefeller walked in a calm and measured manner. Rockefeller stood in front of the counters looking like a small devil from an snuffbox.

Rockefeller had a reputation for being a good owner. He was paid higher salaries than others, provided great pensions, and offered sick days. Rockefeller was determined to prove his point if challenged by subordinates. He was always kind to his subordinates, but they were often afraid of him.

The horror he instilled was shrouded and mysterious. His secretary insists that he has never seen Rockefeller enter or exit the company building. Evidently, he used secret passageways and doors (ill-wishers claimed that a millionaire entered through the chimney).

His house was as frightening as his: simple furnishings, quiet voices. Only the inhabitants knew anything about their daily lives.

Standard Oil Company Oil owner taught his kids music, how-to skate and how to swim. Rockefeller would wake up whenever any of the kids whimpering in the night and make them run for their bed. He was always with his wife and took great care of his mother.

Eliza grew old, became unwell, and Rockefeller rushed to her bedside when she suffered another attack.

Rockefeller reburied his two brothers' children, who died of starvation while they were serving in the Civil War.

"I don't want the monster to lie down in the ground with them!"

But he was very ruthless in business. Rockefeller's capital was estimated to be five million dollars. But, this was not the truth. His company was valued in 1980 at $18,000,000 (the present equivalent is $265,000,000).

Rockefeller became the richest, most powerful person in the country and began an offensive against his competition. He signed an agreement to transport tariffs be inflated with the railway kings.

Rockefeller received their shareholdings from the big capitalists when small oil firms went bankrupt. He soon became a monopolist and was able, in a short time, to set his own prices for oil. This became a strategic commodity during the first half of the twentieth century.

The race began. Great power built ever larger battleships. The fuel they needed was oil.

Standard Oil Company had evolved into a transnational entity. Rockefeller, who was the wealthiest man in the world, had made it possible for his interests to spread around the globe. At the turn century, he was the most wealthy man in the world.

Newspapers reported that Rockefeller owned a fortune of eight and a fifty billion dollars. His monopoly has been called "the greatest and wisest, but most dishonest, of all the things ever made."

Rockefeller knew that by being rich, he was fulfilling God's destiny. This is why, in Protestant ethics wealth was considered a blessing.

His staff recalled the moment when, while they were talking about the grim prospects of the business (it was mentioned that electric lighting might soon replace kerosene), Rockefeller reached for the heavens and said solemnly:

"The God will be there!"

He was careful - the First World War commenced, and all military vessels switched to oil. According to the Protestant Faith, wealth is not something that should be a privilege. Wealth is instead something you have to pay. Rockefeller was able to distribute some of his wealth.

Charity

Be selfless, and help people

-- John D. Rockefeller

Rockefeller had a fortune of thousands and all that money was reinvested in his business. He was now able to give to charity, having amassed hundreds of million.

Rockefeller received over fifty thousand letters within one month, asking for his assistance. He answered every letter and sent checks.

He helped establish the University of Chicago, provided scholarships, and funded pensions. But, all these benefits were actually paid out by the consumers. Rockefeller required them to pay as much for gasoline and Kerosene as the Standard Oil Company>>.

Half of America dreamed to get money from Author. The other half was ready and willing to execute him. Rockefeller grew older and felt the weight of all the pressure. Sometimes, he groaned.

"Wealth can be either a great blessing and a curse."

Rockefeller believed the Standard Oil Company to be an affiliate of God, who drew from the underworld the riches of the Most Great in the form oil and distributed them among the people. Rockefeller chanted, "God bless you, God bless us all Standard Oil!"

A major responsibility was also to raise children. Rockefeller was responsible for the fortune that Rockefeller left his children.

Rockefeller realized that God's gift couldn't be wasted. He taught his kids hard work, modesty, humility, and unpretentiousness.

John Rockefeller Jr. later claimed that in his childhood money was still mysterious to him.

"It was omnipresent but invisible. Although we knew there was plenty of money, we also knew the fact that it was not easily available. "

In fact, the future billionaire stated it with great gentleness for someone who, as a child, wore dresses for boys. Rockefeller's youngest children wore the clothes and styles of their elders. John Rockefeller's oldest son, however, was forced to wear the clothing of his older sisters since they did not have any other boys.

John D. Rockefeller conceived a model to create a market economy at his home. He named Laura his "CEO" (chief executive officer) and instructed his children to keep detailed financial records. Each child got two cents on a dead fly, tencents on sharpening one pencil, or five cents an hour playing music.

A day without chocolate earned two cents. The cost of each day to abstain was approximately ten. Each child had their very own spot in our garden. The ten weeds that were pulled out were worth one dollar.

Rockefeller Jr. earned 15 cents an hr for splitting firewood. The other daughter got money for moving around the house in evenings and dimming lights. The Rockefellers got a one cent penalty for being late for breakfast. They were fined one piece of cheese every day, and banned from reading Sundays except the Bible.

Settie piqued her dresses with her own hands and was not in any way inferior to her husband. Rockefeller, being generously kind, wanted to buy the children bicycles. But his wife said that the additional bikes were not necessary.

"Having four bikes will help them learn to share the bike."

These education results were rather contradictory. Rockefeller Jr. was about to die. As the boy grew older and began to talk about university, he discovered that he was often sick.

John quickly sent his son to a country place, even though the weather was freezing. The sick boy had to rake up stumps, cut down bushes and make wood for his stove. At night, he would shiver from the cold. John survived, graduated from college (he had no money in his pocket and would borrow money from family members) and entered the family enterprise.

John D. Rockefeller deposed his son. His heir lived in his shadow for ever, suffering from this but still faithfully fulfilling his duty. He was a less competent businessman than his father. Newspapers made negative comments about his father. For four long years, he was afraid to tell his lover his feelings.

Johnny Jr. was saved after he married Abby Aldrich. Abby Aldrich (a cheerful and charming little girl) was the daughter from a senator of New York. Her father was a well respected bon vivant. Rockefeller wanted to arrange an alcohol-free nuptial, but her father stated that he would photograph the wedding. The champagne ran like a river, but the Settie of Charity was not there.

John Jr. was taught by Abby how to have fun. John Jr. was in his final term at work. Stock reports caused him to be depressed. But he prospered with his children. John Jr. however raised his offspring as he himself had been raised. Author's unfortunate grandchildren got tenc for every mouse caught.

Rockefeller raising his children had even more devastating consequences. John's older sister Bessie Rockefeller was diagnosed with schizophrenia and spent most her life in bed. After her family went bankrupt, she decided to spend her time making new dresses. Sometimes, she discovered the truth of the matter and informed the nurses with joy that she had money again for her guests.

Edith Rockefeller is an American socialite. She was also an opera patron. At 21 she was suffering from a nervous attack and ended up in hospital. She then married Harold McCormick. McCormick refused a Bible vow that he would never take a drink nor use a card. McCormicks had also been a millionaire. They were strict with children and taught them to aid the poor.

Edith and Harold were an amazing couple. They have squandered several dozen million dollars. Edith discovered the Rockefeller lineage descended from French French aristocrats. She bought an antique chair, coat of arms, and a collection with diamonds. They outperformed the Vanderbilts.

She was always spending money. Edith wore a top-quality silver dress to a ball once. Edith Rockefeller made it clear that she was not interested in meeting her father.

Rockefeller Personal Qualities

Don't be afraid if you have to give up on the good to make way for the great.

-- John D. Rockefeller

Contemporaries were shocked and afraid that John D. Rockefeller had alienated all human life. He distrusted everyone, didn't forgive anyone, was as merciless towards his closest aides as he was to his competitors.

John D. Archibald, who was second in command of company operations, held his right hand. However, even the most powerful businessman trembled before his patron. Archibald was a long-standing Saturday man who submitted to John D. Rockefeller an oath in writing that he had never touched alcohol within the last week.

Rockefeller was famous for his stinginess (as were Andrew Carnegie's and Paul Getty's, Aristotle Onassis and Warren Buffett).

John D. Rockefeller Factory inspected a Standard Oil Company unit that soldered lids for five-gallon cans with kerosene. It was in the 1870s. The future billionaire demanded from the employee who was in charge at Standard Oil Company how many drops of solder were used per lid.

He found out that they had used forty drops. He suggested that they try using 38 drops. These canisters leaked, but canisters sealed by 39 drops turned out to work fine. Rockefeller's calculations show that this saved $2,500 the first season of operation. Profits increased by several hundreds of millions of dollars due to the growth in kerosene exported.

Rockefeller also saved in his personal life. Rockefeller spent time reviewing bills from a grocer, and reduced his supplier's cost from $3,000 - $500 by threatening that he would sue him.

After taxes, his income totaled $50 million. Great golf lover, he insists on using old balls whenever players approach water. He expressed his frustration at the fact people were not afraid to lose their new balls in such situations, and quietly stated:

"They have to be very rich!"

Rockefeller had an ascetic appearance with his egg-shaped bare skull, small eyes, big bat-like ears, thin lips and thin lips. He spoke in a clear and quiet voice, almost without emotion.

His primary concern was the books and accounts. It seemed that way. It wasn't money that worried the magnate. That "something" was his personality.

John D. Rockefeller had two fears that clouded his life: the fear he might lose at least one of his millions of dollars, received not always honestly, and the fear he would lose all of his health.

The last of his fears was eventually defeated. John Rockefeller turned fifty-five in May and was now a "gentleman of the set" businessman. He suffered from a stomach ache and nerve damage. At the suggestion of his doctors, John D. Rockefeller II took over the management of the company and focused solely on treatment.

John D. Rockefeller (18 years old) had set a goal to become the most wealthy man in the world. It was done.

At 55, another goal became a reality: to live to the age of 100. This goal was almost met.

Health Care

It is incorrect to assume that men who have immense wealth are always happy.

-- John D. Rockefeller

John D. Rockefeller resigned from active business in order to achieve a healthy body

& spirit, long-term health, respect for loved ones, and a happy, fulfilling life.

But how does money make all of this possible? They could, it turned to be! That was how he did it.

He attended the Baptist church services every Sunday. There he took notes and tried to apply the principles in everyday life. He slept for 8 hours every night and took a break once a day. He was able get rid of the fatigue and other health problems that were affecting him.

He had a bath or a shower every day, and kept his appearance neat and clean. He moved from California to Florida where the climate is conducive to long-term health. He lived a healthy, balanced lifestyle.

His days were filled playing golf, his favorite game. He enjoyed reading, indoor games, and other positive activities.

He ate slowly, moderately, but thoroughly. This made it easier to absorb and meant that the food was eaten at room temperatures.

He was warned against eating too hot or too cold food, as this could damage the esophagus. He didn't forget vitamins for the spirit and mind. A prayer was said prior to each meal.

Rockefeller was known for asking his secretary or any of the guests or relatives to read the Bible or preach during lunch. Hamilton Fisk Biggar, his doctor full-time, was hired.

Dr. Biggar was paid to make John D. active, happy and healthy. Dr. Biggar achieved this by encouraging his patient to remain positive and energetic. He followed his doctor's advice from the moment he retired to live for 42 more. He died May 23, 1937, from a cardiac arrest at the age of ninety-7.

Rockefeller was a remarkable man, and he lived to be 93 years old.

John D. Rockefeller I, the new head in the dynasty, was a devoted son of his father. He displayed arrogance and cruelty as well as tenacity, resourcefulness and shamelessness. John D. Rockefeller Jr. transformed his father's million dollar business into a multibillionaire.

He opened the way to great wealth with military supplies. The Rockefellers were able to make 500 million dollars in profit from the First World War.

The Second World War proved to have been a profitable business. The demand for gasoline to power aircraft and tank engines made it necessary to have a steady supply of gasoline. This was manufactured at Rockefeller factories that were open 24 hours a day.

Strangely, however, gasoline prices started to rise rapidly. First, by a few Cents per gallon. Then, they increased even more. American soldiers had to use gasoline and other fuel oil for their aircraft, ships, and tanks. Thus, the Rockefeller plants grew in price.

All attempts by the Rockefellers of to argue with them, and appeal to their patriotism were unsuccessful. They replied that they would pay if you needed our products. This resulted in a $2billion net profit during the war years.

Do not mistakenly believe that this story tells the whole story. This is the same story if you read the budget articles about the US military and the statements about Rockefeller firms. Although times have changed, the Rockefellers' morals are the same.

The Rockefellers Today

Is there anything that brings me joy more than seeing my dividends coming in? It's to be able to see my dividends coming back"

-- John D. Rockefeller

Today, five brothers form the family's head: John D. Rockefeller III is 65; Nelson is 63; Lawrence, 61; Winthrop is 59; David, 56; and Abby Aldrich (85), the younger brother of John D. Rockefeller.

Kykuit, New York State, is where four generations are based.

The fourth- and fifth generations of this family are many: several dozen of their grandsons and nephews are descendants of the five siblings. The brothers and their uncle ran the business for years. But they did not advertise their wealth well at one time.

The Rockefellers currently have extravagant homes, yachts, and jewels. But unlike in past times, they don't show it all. They are actually hiding, trying not to seem different from their compatriots. Fear is behind the disguise.

Millionaires had felt fear since October 1917. One of the Rockefeller's official biographers recently wrote:

They could make champagne and place guests on white horses. But they don't.

Although they are rich, some of their behavior is quite remarkable. Lawrence and John D. Rockefeller III will interrupt their lives every morning in order to eat milk and cookies. This is the same as what their father did when he grew up.

All of the Rockefellers, birth to end, live in a world of true royal luxury. John D. Rockefeller Jr., who assured his fellow citizens that humility is essential and that they should expect "divine favor," has so far granted heaven to his five daughters. The Rockefellers are winter residents of New

York, where they live in a nine storey family home.

They have their own clinics, special college, swimming pools and tennis courts. There are also concert and exhibition halls.

David Rockefeller

David has been leading the Rockefeller family from 2004 to now.

His father had 3000 acres of riding and velodromes, a half-million-dollar home theater, a velodrome, and ponds for yacht sailing. The contents of one gaming room alone cost the child-loving oil King 520 thousand Dollars.

Each brother had their own townhouses, summer villas, and other real estate needed for social life as a child. Because the family has so many homes, they often misinterpret their own addresses.

This is not a public announcement, but reporters say that the elder brother teaches his sons how to save money. As a weekly expense rate, the billionaire gave 10 cents to each of these children.

David, who manages the family's wealth management business, says that his only passion is collecting beetles.

David is believed to have 40 million beetles. A businessman makes it possible to take out thousands of people in one day, while collecting his bugs. The press is, however, silent. It's unprofitable for anyone!

The Rockefellers control a multitude of villas as well as palaces. They are thought to be worth hundreds and millions of dollars. About 350 people work at one of these mansions.

The Rockefeller Family has known for many years that the American Government could be used by them to increase income.

John Rockefeller also founded the family business. He realized the value of a friendly person in government to bring in more income that just a few oil fields.

John Rockefeller, the eldest son and heir of his father, was the first to be affected by this "discovery". Old Rockefeller chose the daughter, Senator Nelson Aldrich II, to be his wife. Aldrich was an American political figure who enjoyed long periods of much of the same influence at Washington as the President.

You won't believe it, but Washington hasn't had an administration without a significant number Rockefeller family direct proteges.

The foreign affairs department receives special attention. Rockefeller family members have been in the State Department as the Ministry of Foreign Affairs, which is what America has called it, for many decades.

John Foster Dulles (the same Dulles who became famous for his involvement on the Cold War) is one of Washington's most sinister figures. He was not only an attorney, a legal adviser and a lawyer for Rockefeller's family but also one director of Standard Oil Company.

Dulles came from his position as chairman at the Rockefeller Foundation to join the State Department. This foundation is an influential player in all affairs of the family. Christian Herter, Dulles's successor as foreign secretary, was also closely tied to the Rockefeller firms.

It is hard to imagine that Dean Rusk, who was previously the Rockefeller Foundation chairman, would be the Secretary-of-State in the Kennedy or Johnson administrations.

The oil magnates have lost their direct, but real, access to the government for some time. In recent decades, the Rockefellers have made multiple attempts to grab key government positions.

One of five brothers, Winthrop ROCKELFeller, decided that he would run for Arkansas governor during 1964's election campaign. The economic prospect of capturing the governor's chair was promising and rich. Additionally, the state promised significant benefits to the Rockefellers. Thus, the brothers spent all their money on Winthrop's election campaign.

WinthropRockefeller as a newcomer on the political scene, did not get elected to the governor's position. This failure didn't discourage him.

WinthropRockefeller, having spent several hundred thousand dollars, got his way to the governor's house in the capital city of Arkansas. Winthrop was elected governor of Arkansas. He also served as chairman of Colonial Williamsburg.

John Davison Rockefeller IV of the fourth generation, was elected as the Virginia congressman in the fall of 1966.

Nelson, Rockefeller Jr.'s only son, was born on the exact same day as his famous grandfather.

John D. Rockefeller II was the Rockefeller Foundation chairman. This foundation collected one of the best collections of Asian art and also funded New York's Lincoln Center for Fine Arts. David was chairman of Chase Manhattan Bank (a Rockefeller family project) and chairman of Museum of Modern Art.

Lawrence, a well-known conservationist and philanthropist, donated the land from which the Virgin Islands National Park later was established.

The "Rockefeller people", John Dulles, Dean Acheson, Dean Rusk, Henry Kissinger, Zigmund Brüzezinski have held the helm of American power for the past ten years.

The Rockefellers shared the "spheres of impact" in the state apparatus. Nelson & John were "friends," Lawrence with Pentagon, David with Ministry of Finance and Lawrence with State Department. The Brothers never paid too much for "friendly" services.

It was known that Henry Kissinger was given a "gift", in the form of 50 000 dollars by the Rockefellers, when he was appointed to the position of national security adviser.

Others received "gifts" up to 120 million, 40 000, 75 thousand, 230 thousand, and other amounts.

John D. Rockefeller , who directed large amounts of money towards helping people, became a legend.

He was a teenager when he gave money to a Baptist parish. John was able give out as much money as he earned after becoming rich.

Rockefeller and several of his foundations have donated more that 530,000,000 dollars to charity over his lifetime. This is an enormous fortune, but it's still a significant amount today.

The University of Chicago received $35 million from Rockefeller. Rockefeller Sanitary Commission was able to distribute tens of thousands pairs of shoes which destroyed ankilostomidosis.

The Institute of Medical Research opened in Rockefeller's name. It was the very first institute that was created solely for medical research. The facility enabled research into and treatment for serious diseases.

Many friends report that John D. Rockefeller maintained an interest in the business throughout his life. However, his business activities were restricted to advising John Rockefeller Jr. (and other business leaders). Author died in 1937, just before he turned 98.

Rockefeller has a profound influence on US history that is hard to overestimate. He is the only person who actually built the country's oil industry. His Standard Oil Company gave birth to most of the US's modern oil companies. His capital is estimated to have been between $190 and 320 billion in today's dollars. Some of his contemporaries considered him a monopolist and called him a cruel businessman. Now, he's recognized as one if the United States' founding fathers, one of the greatest entrepreneurs, and a key influence on the incredible growth of the oil sector.

John D. Rockefeller is a great success

Dates from John D. Rockefeller's biography:

* 1839 babies born

* 1843 opened his first business

* 1856 got his job

* 1864 Marriage to S. Spelman

* 1870 established an oil company

* 1880 consolidated almost all oil output in its possession

* 1892 founded University of Chicago

* 1901 created a medical college, the Rockefeller University

* 1913 founded Rockefeller Foundation

* 1935 was recognized by the insurance company with a cash reward as a long-liver.

* 1937, a victim of heart failure.

Some interesting facts about John D. Rockefeller

* He was one of the richest men in the world

* He was more than 2% America's GDP

* He owned many businesses

* All US oil companies now count their activities starting with John D. Rockefeller

* Owned 50% or more of the global crude oil market

* His main charitable recipients were the Church as well as educational institutions

* Financed the study one type of deadly flu.

* Didn't die only three years before his 100th birth.

* John D. Rockefeller's five grandsons became prominent politicians as well as benefactors.

* UN headquarters were built because John D. Rockefeller donated $6 Million towards its construction.

* Rockefeller's son constructed the Empire State Building which is the most famous skyscraper of all time.

* John Rockefeller was called "Rockefelia" in honor of the 1918 discovery of an asteroid.

* John and Mary lived together for over 60+ years. Laura Spelman Rockefeller Memorial Fund was established in her honour by Rockefeller. This foundation is still active and deals with issues related to education and fights against racial discrimination.

1 Redeeming the FamilyName

"I believe in individual worth and the right to live, liberty, and pursue happiness. I believe that each right involves a responsibility, every opportunity, an obligation, and every possession, a burden.

- Stanzas I & 2 from the Credo of Author

Rockefeller's name is synonymous with America's wealth and power. It is however not a name that is well-respected. Rockefeller, despite its apparent endless wealth and seemingly limitless funds, was still a name associated to unethical monopoly as well as the widespread mistreatment and abuse of workers who supported it. Author, was one of many who are often called the "Robber Barons," or American Industrial Age.

The family fortune started when Rockefeller founded the Standard Oil Company in Ohio in 1870. So-named because Senior Rockefeller had high standards. He expected his company would be a beacon of quality and customer service. But, soon, the group also demonstrated that they were willing to follow less-admirable standards to ensure corporate efficiency. Rockefeller Senior along with his associates recognized the financial benefits of streamlining operations. Standard Oil consolidated all aspects, including refining and distribution. Rockefeller Senior began purchasing suppliers, gaining control over processing facilities, as well as buying out distribution partners. Standard Oil became more aggressive in buying smaller companies, and eventually absorbed rival companies. Standard Oil lost many jobs and gained a reputation that was ruthless and uncaring in its business dealings. Rockefeller Senior was as ruthless and Standard Oil could expand their international operations by exporting to China first, then expanding to other nations.

The American public became angry at their unbalanced approach, which led to the closure of many businesses. Although the business theory proved to have been sound and had produced unquestionable benefits for its investors, it soon caused outrage. Standard Oil's unrivalled size, scope and ability to get tax advantages, legal protections, huge corporate discounts and enormous corporate discounts further fuelled public outrage. A combination of financial and competitive advantages made it impossible to find other oil companies any place in the market. Standard Oil had already established a monopoly that controlled the prices and profits. They no more had to uphold high standards of service and quality towards their employees. Even worse, labor disputes started quickly.

The Standard Oil Trust would be targeted by allegations of unfair labor practices as well as mounting pressure on government officials for fairness through legislation. The Supreme Court would dissolve the well-structured trust into 34 smaller companies in 1911 by adopting anti-trust legislation.

Rockefeller believed that it was his responsibility to build such wealth, despite all of the public outrage over the unfair monopoly. He believed, and often acted upon, his bound obligation to assist worthy causes, as well as alleviating the burdens of those less privileged than himself. This was such an integral part of his being that he read every request for financial aid, interviewed each person he was interested in granting funds to and distributed the funds himself. But, philanthropic ventures were time-consuming and hindered his focus on the business.

Author Jr., a young man who had been raised as his father's child, stepped in to help. He was taught the values of efficiency, and how to run a business. He had been taught to value money and the need for close management. He was taught to value the Baptist beliefs of father. This was evident even while he served as an instructor at Brown University. While he was responsible for leading Bible studies, he also showed great control over his finances. Junior, who had graduated from Brown University on May 18, 1897, joined his father in the business world as a director of Standard Oil's New York headquarters.

His father's personality was evident while he worked in the family business. Rockefeller was competent in his director role and fully capable in performing the duties. However he found little joy or fulfillment in business that focuses on making money and engineering business transactions. His passion was in giving away the wealth he inherited from his family. For him, it was the exact task that was the burden on his father's shoulders that provided the source of his life. Senior recognized an answer to his overwhelming workload, as well as an opportunity for him to salvage the reputation and name of Standard Oil Company. Senior swiftly appointed Junior in the newly created position of Chief at the Rockefeller Foundation. The foundation is purely philanthropic. The lessons of religion & piety that his father understood through the lenses of duty and obligation towards lesser humanity, Author, turned into lessons that taught him compassion and generosity. His sense of duty and obligation to the Northern Baptist Church would not lead him to philanthropy. But he would have a wellspring in his soul that would allow him to feel righteous and humbled to be trusted with the responsibility of serving humanity in this capacity.

Author, Jr., a man who was finding his calling, Author Jr. would restore the Rockefeller brand, provide relief and resources to laborers, educate and provide medical care for the nation, protect natural treasures for American posterity, reaffirm his Credo, and eventually, be buried on the wall of his alma maternity.

2 Of Law and Labor

"I believe the law is made for man, and not man for it; the government is the servant to the people, and not their master. I believe in the dignity that comes with labor, no matter how it is done. It does not owe any one a living, but everyone an opportunity to make a living.

- Stanzas 3. & 4. of The Credo of Author.

Junior, who was content to stay behind-the scenes of his father's expanding company and faithfully distributed the Rockefeller Foundation's huge wealth to worthy causes large or small, would eventually be thrust into the spotlight and establish him as the public, humanizing face the Rockefeller fortune.

Far from New York, in Colorado's mining country was a small settlement called Ludlow. The Colorado Fuel and Iron Corporation (a Rockefeller holding, of which Junior was an unspoken director and 40% shareholder), owned the Ludlow, a mining community that quickly became a hotbed for labor dissent. The mines' unsafe conditions and long working hours were not tolerated by company representatives. Miners protesting the increase in wealth of corporate bosses and the hardships faced by their families in towns run by them decided to strike. The Ludlow miners quit their jobs in September 1913.

The bold statement by miners did little to encourage dialogue from Colorado Fuel and Iron Corporation. Instead, they escalated tensions by evicting miners and their families. This power of the corporation over every aspect their lives was exactly what sparked the strike. It did nothing but anger the miners and bolster their resolve. The United Mine Workers Union offered emergency support and the unaffected strikers set up tent camps just outside the company town. They continued their protest against poor living conditions, unsafe working conditions, and other unfair conditions.

All of this was happening without the knowledge and approval of Junior Rockefeller. He had little interest in the business he had built his wealth. He left these matters to others, and remained centered on his philanthropic work. However, further escalation would force him to pay attention.

Ludlow (Colorado) company bosses were faced with a hillside full if belligerently striking miners who were tent-occupying and fighting for their rights. They decided to forcibly expel the families. The Rockefeller officials in Colorado weren't interested in reaching a compromise. They believed that the miners were under no personal responsibility and hired the Baldwin-Felts Detective Agency. The agency was empowered to use all necessary means and raided a camp with Gatlin guns. It also used extreme force to kill many miners.

Despite the murderous plans of the Colorado Fuel and Iron Corporation, the miners refused the invitation to surrender. Their cause wasn't just. It was about much more than themselves. These miners would stand firm in the face of similar conditions in their company towns. They would keep their strike going and be heard. With the conviction that they were on right side, miners were encouraged by the Colorado National Guard. With the Guard's protection, it was clear that there would no more violence towards them. This would allow the company to strike and force them to negotiate.

To the shock and dismay the miners, it became apparent that the National Guard had not intended to protect the families of the miners from undue violent acts. The Guard, which had been called in at the request the Colorado Fuel and Iron Corporation by the governor, was actually responsible for escalating the violence. Again, the Rockefeller monopoly's power was used to destroy those who were in its path. The National Guard soldiers repeatedly raided this camp, killing miners and taking others into custody. They became the victim of a prolonged, full-scale assault. But the miners refused give up and continued to fight. They lost more numbers after being out-gunned. They kept fighting, believing these actions only confirmed the urgency and importance of their cause.

Month after mois passed with no decreases in tensions. Month after moist passed without Author speaking up about company activities. He prefered to keep this to his employees. Junior Rockefeller was not the only one to be affected by the events of April 20, 1914. The entire nation would have to pay attention. Shortly after dawn, National Guard troops entered the miners' encampment to open fire on the tents. The miners' leader, in desperate need of stopping the carnage and approaching the National Guard for help, was shot without warning. Panicked, the children, women, and men hid beneath their tents in the hope of escaping the bullets. The Guard reacted and set fire at the entire encampment.

As it was called, the Ludlow Massacre would lead to a civil war between labor organizations and the company. The United Mine Workers Union created a militia with 300 men, armed them and marched to Ludlow. It caused chaos in the mines and killed guards. Following their compatriots' deaths, the Ludlow miners took up arms and joined forces. Colorado National Guard soldiers refused orders to deploy, citing the unwillingness to join the murder of innocents. The public protested across the nation, outraged at the injustice and demanded that it be addressed. Finally, President Woodrow Wilson was asked to intervene, directing federal resources for restoring order. The fighting was over, the troops returned to their homes, but there was no progress.

The entire incident polarized the public more towards the unfair monopoly and violent opposition of ultra-rich corporations to any sense that they had of responsibility to their workers. Junior Rockefeller had to stop turning a blindeye and voicing his disgust at the actions of his colleagues. Junior took a trip himself to Ludlow because he became aware of all the injustice that was going against everything he believed. He sat down alongside the workers. He listened carefully to the complaints made by the miners. The media and miners both were skeptical about this gesture. They were shocked at the next thing.

Junior Rockefeller proved to have a character far greater than what they imagined. He was more than a corporate head with no empathy, who strove to be disconnected and immoral in order to benefit the laborers. He heard them. He realized his past inadequacy in paying attention to the affairs and businesses that bore his name. He was disgusted over the abuses of power. He recognized that a business has the right not to be governed by its employees but he said that the business must treat its employees with equity.

Junior took up Junior's cause of an 8-hour week. He spoke in support of safe workplaces and a standard for living that must not be compromised. His own words:

My belief has been held firm for many years that employers as well as employees are partners. They share the same interests and are in common. The success of both is dependent on the success in the long term. If the labor force will contribute to industrial warfare being outlawed; substituting partnership accordingly; if more men are broad-sighted and have high goals, it may be possible for the trade unionism movement to enjoy the glory of ushering peace in the industrial sector.

3 Economy and Expanding

"I believe that thrift can be essential to well-ordered lifestyle and that a strong financial structure is a prerequisite for sound government, business, and personal finances."

Stanza 5 to the Credo for Author

Junior Rockefeller learned thrift and economy from a young age. They were values he saw in his father. Like many of his generation and others, Author had learned from an early age the importance of hard work as well as stretching pennies. Senior

Rockefeller, the son of a farmer started at the tender age of 16 as a produce clerk for the local grocer. He had already started his business venture with a friend at the age of nineteen. His main responsibilities were to handle the banking and office affairs. Rockefeller is most well-known for the Standard Oil Company. This first company earned a handsome profit in its first years. Rockefeller wasn't like other business tycoons who took this steady profitability as an invitation to indulge.

The lessons learned by his father in regards to wealth were passed on to the younger Rockefeller. Junior Rockefeller's home was not the 5th Avenue residence of his peers. It was not an extravagant estate, designed by a single person and filled with the most current finery. It was actually an old brownstone residence that the previous owners had modified, but whose original appointments remained intact when the Rockefellers bought it. The home was conveniently located in New York to allow Standard Oil to conduct its business. It was large enough to accommodate all of the family's needs. Local reporter, who was visiting the home at the time, noted that there were only a few servants, compared to the full-time staff that Rockefeller had. Additionally, the family had their own housekeeping duties. "He puts on not much ..."," he states, almost stunned, as he adds, "He claims no praises for getting rich and sticks loyally to Dr. Armitage's Baptist Church. Of which he am a member."

Junior Rockefeller grew to be a man of great wealth, but he also had great humility. Although he had a better home than his father he made sure to avoid the indulgences that his fellow ranks enjoyed. This financial discipline carried over to his business and charitable activities. While giving was the greatest joy of his existence, he was careful to make sure that every dollar received was used to its highest value. This is most evident in his transactions with the Grand Teton National Park.

Junior Rockefeller loved national beauty and was captivated by it. He was passionate about natural vistas and believed that they were an escape from everyday life. His mission was to make sure these kinds of retreats are available to all Americans. Junior became determined to stop commercial development from taking over the Grand Teton National Park. This land was also valuable to the commercial sector, which he quickly realized. To preserve the land without losing his determination to not overspend would require all his skill.

Rockefeller sought to find the right balance between expansion and thrift, and soon came up with a plan. Rockefeller would first purchase the land from the nearby commercial property and then donate them to National Park Service in order to incorporate them into National Park holdings. Andrew White, Park Services spokesperson notes that he was "willing" to pay fair-market values for the land, however not Rockefeller. Other concerns were the possible pushback by other companies if the land was removed from commercial usage. Rockefeller tried to get out of the equation and ensure market pricing was not affected by his millionaire status. To hide the intent from developers, he formed Snake River Land Company. This company purchased all of the surrounding parcels at fair prices through agents. Competitors and locals eager for new commercial ventures only realized the truth after the deals were closed.

Area ranchers were furious at the loss. They had been fighting a bitter fight over the original 29,000 acres, which were designated in 1929 as national park land. This was before the addition of the 35,000 acres Rockefeller Land. Developers who believed they had the land stolen from under them brought suit (all of which were unsuccessful). Local government officials tried to prevent Junior Rockefeller gifting the land to Federal Government. The plan angered the constituents of Wyoming, and the Wyoming congressmen fought to stop any acceptance by the National Parks Service.

Junior wanted to see an end to fifteen years of legal and politically tangled political debates. He devised a careful plan to save money and to give back to the community to support his conservation and philanthropic missions. But it wasn't cost-effective or efficient to start conservation efforts. He took a bold step and went straight to Franklin Delano Roosevelt. Rockefeller demanded that Roosevelt either solve the problem or locate the gifted lands. Junior wouldn't hesitate selling them to anyone and everything was over. The threat was enough to force Franklin Delano Roosevelt to sign the executive order that established the Jackson Hole Monument. Further protests ensued. Opposing bills were introduced and blocked. The matter would remain unresolved until 1950, when Harry Truman, another President, would sign an order merging 1929's park lands with 1943's addition of the Jackson Hole Monument. This would create the Grand Teton National Park today, which covers 310,000 acre and includes a highway linking Grand Teton to Yellowstone.

One wonders if Junior would have preferred transparency and openness to his core economic intent of thrift and entrepreneurship at the beginning of this venture. The lands were nevertheless obtained and established for their intended purpose. And all at "fair-market" and not "Rockefeller prices.

4 The centrality of integrity

"I believe in the fundamental importance of justice and truth for a sustainable social order. I believe in a sacredness to a promise. A man's bond should be as good a word as his word. It is character that is most important, and not wealth, power, or position.

- Stanzas 6, 7 and 8 of The Credo of Author.

Junior Rockefeller's actions show a deep belief that integrity is the thread running through them all. It is often said that one can't really believe something unless it manifests in his actions. Junior has demonstrated through his actions that his Credo transcends mere words. Each of these principles is founded on sound character, justice, and truth.

This underpinning belief was not only his. Junior was driven to instill this quality of character, integrity and selflessness in others through the causes and organizations he supported. Again, his philanthropic efforts followed his values.

Junior made a huge donation and formed a close friendship with Boy Scouts of America to ensure that a next generation of integrity and character was raised. Junior experienced as a boy the joy of camping, riding on horses through the wild, and learning self-sufficiency. He realized that many young men did not have such opportunities to build their character. Junior recognized that the Boy Scouts was an organization that would offer these opportunities to young American men. He was fully supportive of the cause. They didn't care about their economic status; their value was determined not by what they owned or their ability make money but by the character they developed while participating in Boy Scouts.

Junior Rockefeller made a commitment to Boy Scouts during his long friendship. He donated not only funds but also lands.

Junior also purchased lands in New York and New Jersey in an identical fashion to his Grand Teton purchase. These lands, now known as the Alpine Camp were then donated to Boy Scouts as a camping ground. Andrew Nichols - director of camping - praised Rockefeller and said it answered one of New York's most pressing questions: "How do we provide outdoor experiences and activities for New York City Scouts at low transport costs and accessible for day or weekend use " The potential development of this site, with its proximity to the Palisades Interstate Park and its extensiveness, is endless.

Junior Rockefeller understood that character and integrity could not be reserved for the next generation. In fact, he encouraged the growth of truth and justice in existing educational and governmental institutions. Believing that justice was well-served by an understanding of history, he once again secretly purchased historically-relevant lands in Colonial Williamsburg, Virginia, preserving them for the purpose of establishing a living-history tableau that would instruct both current citizens and coming generations in the history of the United States. His goal was for the courage, the demand for justice and the action motivated by true-held values to inspire a continuation in the spirit that inspired our forefathers.

The most well-known gesture in his pursuit for truth and justice for America, as well as for the establishment of an international initiative toward these noble ideals, was the 16-acre donation of New York land for the United Nations Headquarters. Junior Rockefeller style. He purchased the 18-acre land in prime New York territory through thrifty money from a developer who was short of cash. This purchase was as philosophical as it was philanthropic. Rockefeller was determined at the heart of the greatest American city to unite world powers. A political noman's country, none owned by any country, all powers holding each other in respect & equality, all joining together to improve the lives of mankind; this was Junior's highest expression for the rule o truth, justice and integrity.

Junior Rockefeller managed to achieve a wide range of accomplishments, from local, small-scale projects to global philanthropies. This was all while remaining a man with the same integrity that he hoped others would emulate. Rockefeller was more than a philosopher. He lived and breathed philosophy and invested in its values. Truth. Justice. Honesty over power. He was a firm believer in these principles to the point of taking action.

5 Supremacy of Selflessness

"I believe that the rendering useful service of mankind is the common deed of man and that only in sacrifice is the dross selfishness consumed and human greatness set free."

Stanza 8 of The Credo of Author

Author, while not a millionaire, did not live in isolation from society. He was surrounded by people of his education, opportunity, wealth and status. He had a bigger and more luxuriously decorated home than his dad, but he always tried to connect to those in their lives so they could be of service to humanity. He lived his life with an open mind to the suffering and sought to assist when it was possible. It was a simple act American citizenship which would allow him to see an epidemic problem right in his backyard, and help to motivate his efforts to right this great injustice.

Junior was elected to be foreman at Supreme Court proceedings in 1910 concerning what was called "white slavery"; what we now call prostitution. During these proceedings the desperate conditions of those living with this way of earning their living were revealed to him.

Rockefeller, shocked by the human suffering, was inspired to establish the Bureau of Social Hygiene, which was established in 1911.

Rockefeller funds financed the Bureau, which began investigating a wide range of social problems related to prostitution. In order to prevent young people from being prostitution-trapped, programs were developed to teach high school students about the dangers posed by narcotics, encourage productive use in school, and provide education on sexual health. In order to improve their chances of prosecuting and exposing corruption in their police departments, the Bureau collaborated with them to investigate and understand prostitution rings. To help those who have been caught in prostitution's trap, medical research was conducted as well as efforts to provide treatment for venereal disease sufferers.

Junior's Bureau of Social Hygiene established venereology, an entire branch of medicine. His interests in medical research, health care, and the establishment hospitals would never cease.

Rockefeller's work with Bureau came to an abrupt halt in 1930. A new avenue of useful service to humanity would open up in the Great Depression. Americans were mostly without work and projects that had been begun before the economic collapse were frozen. Junior Rockefeller, who was one of few men with remaining substantial financial resources began to contemplate how he could most effectively use those resources to help. Rockefeller realized that a nation devoid of hope, without employment, and with a loss of sight of beauty was a country in crisis. He decided to make a comeback by building his "city inside a city," which is the Rockefeller Center.

Junior's vision wasn't just to create the jobs necessary to get the project off the ground, but also to provide a platform for businesses to start over and to showcase the beauty of art again. Rockefeller Center provided a great service to the American people when it was opened in 1933. It became a refuge from the harsh reality of economic collapse. Its walls were covered in art. The theaters also hosted art. Booksellers and newspapers provided words of hope, and also offered opportunities. Christmas tree lightings lifted spirits. Rockefeller's cash assets were sacrificed in order to help New Yorkers escape the Great Depression's despairing prison.

Junior would once more allow the conditions he saw around his to motivate him to give useful service to those who had sacrificed their lives in World War II. Recognizing the need for meaningful work for returning soldiers, the burden of their experiences, and their desire to find nondestructive outlets of their energy, the Rockefeller fortune was once tapped again to create the United Service Organizations.

Like all Junior's projects before it, the USO would research the best ways to use the money. Junior's initial studies on the needs of returning soldiers were a strong indicator that the USO would not allow ineffective spending. This helped to ensure that the funds went to the best activities and projects. Surprisingly soldiers did not seek out companionship or frivolous entertainment. It was jobs that would provide something of value to others. Music that would broaden and enrich their tastes. Education for the different world where they were returning. The USO provided everything you need: job training programs; hobby clubs; music and dancehalls that play all styles of music. Junior's Bureau of Social Hygiene had taught him a lot about venereal disease. The USO would provide education about the importance of proper sexual and health care.

Junior Rockefeller was not able to sacrifice anything financial - his accounts were filled as fast and empty as his treasures. However, it is evident that he lived an exemplary life and did everything in his power to remove himself from any problems. To improve the lives and well-being of others, he deliberately chose to make his life uncomfortable. He took on immense tasks. To liberate others from their hopelessness, sickness and poverty.

6 Religion beyond mere duty

"I believe there is an all-wise and loving God. Living in harmony with Him will bring you the greatest fulfillment, happiness, and most usefulness.

Stanza 9 of The Credo of Author

Junior's Christian faith was shaped within the Baptist tradition of his father. While he continued to adhere to the Baptist faith of his childhood, he eventually left the denomination. Junior, a firm believer, in prayer, Bible studies, and the application Christian principles to every aspect of life - service and duty, love, among other things - grew increasingly disillusioned by the Northern Baptist Convention of the which his family had been a member. The more he studied the world and participated in its alleviation through philanthropy the more convinced was he that unity among Christians, even though he held unity between nations, was the only way for his church to make a positive impact on it. He summarized his belief in 1937 radio speech as "Only a united Christian World can stem the rising tides materialism, selfishness and programs; hobby clubs; music and dancehalls that play all styles of music. Junior's Bureau of Social Hygiene had taught him a lot about venereal disease. The USO would provide education about the importance of proper sexual and health care.

Junior Rockefeller was not able to sacrifice anything financial - his accounts were filled as fast and empty as his treasures. However, it is evident that he lived an exemplary life and did everything in his power to remove himself from any problems. To improve the lives and well-being of others, he deliberately chose to make his life uncomfortable. He took on immense tasks. To liberate others from their hopelessness, sickness and poverty.

6 Religion beyond mere duty

"I believe there is an all-wise and loving God. Living in harmony with Him will bring you the greatest fulfillment, happiness, and most usefulness.

Stanza 9 of The Credo of Author

Junior's Christian faith was shaped within the Baptist tradition of his father. While he continued to adhere to the Baptist faith of his childhood, he eventually left the denomination. Junior, a firm believer, in prayer, Bible studies, and the application Christian principles to every aspect of life - service and duty, love, among other things - grew increasingly disillusioned by the Northern Baptist Convention of the which his family had been a member. The more he studied the world and participated in its alleviation through philanthropy the more convinced was he that unity among Christians, even though he held unity between nations, was the only way for his church to make a positive impact on it. He summarized his belief in 1937 radio speech as "Only a united Christian World can stem the rising tides materialism, selfishness and crumbling moral standard, and point out the way."

Junior knew that recognizing this philosophy was not sufficient to make him a good person. He began looking for ways to make Christianity a reality, recognizing that this was the best way to live in peace with God. The Institute of Social and Religious Research was created out of this compulsion. To study the role and structure of the church in society, academics were brought together. The objective was to scientifically examine how the morality, ethics, or organizational structures of the church could better guide positive outcomes for society. This was revolutionary work, since the relationship between religions and the study of the social sciences was unknown at the time.

While the work was controversial, the Institute's analyses and reports formed the basis for what we now refer to as the Social Gospel. We believe that Christianity is best expressed through the use of social programs.

The research from 1921-1934 led to the discovery that modern-day churches operate soup kitchens. Junior Rockefeller's vision, funding and willingness to collaborate, along with other social scientists, made huge strides in social assistance from a Christian perspective.

Rockefeller believed, along with the church's responsibility to interact with society that the church needed break down religious and faith barriers in order for the church and the world to be a force for good. He did not care who God was, just that he existed. He believed that the church should work together under the banners divine good to eradicate the evil and ills plaguing the world. This belief is sometimes called "ecumenicalism" within religious circles.

Author, held the traditional Protestant views and was not a follower of the ecumenical ideas of his son. He gave a lot of money to Northern Baptist projects throughout his life. In fact, he founded the University of Chicago to be an Baptist theological seminary. Junior would also follow these footsteps, and he was the single largest North Baptist donor for many years. As the institution grew, however, there was growing discord between the Baptists' traditional views and the Modernists. Junior's beliefs were more closely aligned to those of the Modernists. They split from Northern Baptists in the end over their irreconcilable divergences. It's hard to miss the irony in refusing reconciliation among a group that claimed unity is the only solution for the good of all the world.

Junior left the Northern Baptists. His support for religious initiatives grew, including the establishment of Riverside Church, which was a nondenominational Church. There were also large donations to Interchurch World Movement. Junior sought to bring together all religions for the common benefit. He was also known for sending millions of dollars to Jewish- and Roman Catholic programs that provided housing, education, medical care, as well as biblical teachings to Asia or Africa.

Junior valued unity. It was not just unity in religion, but unity across all races. Unification becomes the rallying song and discrimination is not tolerated in any corner. Junior was determined to foster harmony between races. He became the champion of the International House New York. Although this may sound like a simple vision, the International House was able to accomplish exactly what its name indicates. It houses international students from universities around New York City. Students of 100 different nationalities are able to live, learn, eat, and study with each other under the inscription, "That Brotherhood may Prevail."

Author, Jr. believed it was an ineffective, empty religion that did little to alleviate suffering and unify humanity. He didn't discriminate about the banner that was used for the work. As long as the work was done, he was willing and able to provide financial support. Junior saw this as his highest calling. He believed it was his ultimate harmony and the will of Go.

Printed by Libri Plureos GmbH in Hamburg, Germany